50 MISTAKES BUSINESS OWNERS MAKE

By

Marcus Guiliano
Business Coach, International Speaker,
Owner/Executive Chef Aroma Thyme Bistro

&

Carl Solomon, M.S.Ed.

Copyright © 2017

50 Mistake Business Owners Make

For information contact:

Marcus@MarcusGuiliano.com

www.50Mistakes.com

Book and Cover design by Perry Elisabeth Design

perryelisabethdesign.com

ISBN-13: 978-1541389786

First Edition: January 2017

10 9 8 7 6 5 4 3 2 1

TABLE OF CONTENTS

Foreword i

Preface..iii

Acknowledgments...v

Introduction..1

I.   Guest Relations 6

Mistake #1: You're not collecting guest data................................6

Mistake #2: You don't use in-house comment cards....................8

Mistake #3: Don't let your guests forget about you...................10

Mistake #4: Your follow-up sucks...12

Mistake #5: You don't have a loyalty program..........................15

Mistake #6: You don't keep or appropriately use your database................17

Mistake #7: How to get a guest to spend $5K? You don't know the value of a "lifetime" guest. 19

Mistake #8: You don't understand the value of paying to get new guests.23

Mistake #9: You don't know how to use social media to your advantage..25

II.   Business Operations 30

Mistake #10: You don't have a website or don't maintain the one you have. 30

Mistake #11: Gee, that empty restaurant sure looks like fun!....................34

Mistake #12: You don't grow your sales......................................36

Mistake #13: You don't avail yourself of those who've gone before you. The highest form of flattery is… 39

Mistake #14: You don't have a clue about how your vendors are charging you. 41

Mistake #15: You don't keep tabs on your business. 46

Mistake #16: You don't respond to the good. 50

Mistake #17: Your staff doesn't know how to ask questions. 52

Mistake #18: You don't answer the phone when it rings. Pick it up! 55

Mistake #19: You don't have a guarantee of satisfaction or your money back policy. 58

Mistake #20: Cross Promoting: You don't leverage your confidence with other local businesses. 61

Mistake #21: You don't have an opening line. You lose them at hello. 65

Mistake #22: You haven't turned the light on in the room yet...support locally. 68

Mistake #23: Horse trading is back. Do you know how to barter? 71

Mistake #24: You've forgotten how to play like a kid in a candy store. Go to a trade show or two. 73

Mistake #25: Reading is definitely fundamental. Read those trade books and other related publications. 75

Mistake #26: You don't have the confidence to talk to your competition. ... 77

Mistake #27: You don't participate in community service. 80

Mistake #28: You don't require a jacket and tie, so why is your food wrapped in that attire? 83

Mistake #29: You don't have the skill to market for new staff. 86

Mistake #30: Interviewing: You don't know how to hold an audition. 89

Mistake #31: Performance Reviews. You don't know how to be honest with your staff. 94

Mistake #32: You don't take advantage of instant replay: check those references. 97

Mistake #33: You don't invest in your largest expense by training your staff. 99

Mistake #34: You don't take time out to play with your staff. 103

III.   Advertising/Promotion **105**

Mistake #35: You don't have a billboard. 105

Mistake #36: You don't know how or when to tell a good story. 107

Mistake #37: Your guests don't really know who you are. 110

Mistake #38: You blew your entire advertising budget in one place. 113

IV.   Cooking **115**

Mistake #39: Your regular menu gets boring. 115

Mistake #40: You're the best chef in town, but this doesn't qualify you to run a successful business. Cooking should be the last part of your job. 118

Mistake #41: You think people get their vitamins and fiber at home. 121

Mistake #42: Your bar looks like a big box store midnight sale. 125

V.   Personal Growth **128**

Mistake #43: Hey hothead, do you react or do you respond? 128

Mistake #44: You don't tell the truth, the whole truth and nothing but the truth. 133

Mistake #45: You don't know how to say no. Try it sometimes, it feels good. 136

Mistake #46: You don't wait 24 hours before responding to irrationality. 138

Mistake #47: You don't have the support you need. 141

Mistake #48: Great minds do think alike but you're not a Mastermind...yet. 143

Mistake #49: Your job description has become a monster growing out of control. You need to learn to trust your staff. 147

Mistake #50: You're at the bottom of your own list. You need to refill your own cup. 151

Foreword

HEY BUSINESS OWNER! Are you on a mission in your business? Is it serving you and your family - or are you a slave to the business - working days, nights, weekends and holidays?

Are you ready to up-level your day-to-day activity, to become more profitable, fall in love with your business again and rediscover your life with your family and your personal interests? Take a really deep breath. While you may be overdue for a vacation and the idea of it may be a shock; it is definitely with the realm of possibility. Oh, and if the idea of leaving your staff in charge of your business gives you the willies...well take another deep breath and read on. I've known Marcus Guiliano for a number of years and I can tell you he's been on both sides of this scenario, as I have as well. You can trust the advice provided here and begin visualizing that vacation. In fact, use the visualization as part of your motivating fuel.

If you want to be in a position to buy what you want, when you want, either for business upgrades, training or equipment or your life and your family, then I suggest you read *50 Mistakes Business Owners Make*.

You can only do more both personally and professionally with a profitable business. Conversely you cannot, if you're making mistakes in: guest/customer relations; business operations; advertising/promotion; hiring practices; cooking; maintaining a solid database; and even in areas of personal growth. Since you've been led to be holding this book in your hands you are clearly one of those business professionals who is open to some input. Congratulations. Being open to hearing what it takes to grow puts you in rather unique class of business owners. You know you don't know everything and need guidance, and perhaps even some coaching to become stronger in the areas you're currently not an expert. There are precious few who don't need a coach. From Hall of Famers to weekend warriors, mentorship, coaching, guidance, or expert advice is what gets that individual to the next level of success and expertise. So, why do you think you're any different?

Take your turn because your time is now.

Whether you're the business owner, manager, key employee, or someone even lower in the hierarchy, but you have a desire to see more, do more, and bring that something extra to the table, then *50 Mistakes Business Owners Make* is your path to the next level. So…what are you waiting for?

Misty Young
Co-Founder/CEO: YoungSocial.com

Preface

IT IS IMPORTANT, NO, actually critical the reader understand the perspective from which the following work was conceived and written. My working orientation, understanding, and success as a business owner: centers on owning and operating a restaurant. My background is steeped in many kitchens and dining rooms of restaurants across the country as a chef/employee and across the world as a researcher/guest/observer. I have been somewhat obsessed with the pursuit of not only perfecting my craft, but owing to some personal health issues, the pursuit of healing those concerns naturally and through the use of wholesome foods. This ultimately led to the creation of Aroma Thyme Bistro. As of this writing we're in our 14th year and more successful than we've ever been.

Through the many trade-shows, conferences, and mastermind seminars we've attended over the years, I recently came to understand that I have a deeply growing passion to help others succeed in their business. Additionally, distilling a great many learning opportunities (read into that: successes and failures) at Aroma Thyme Bistro; I truly desire to share what I've learned to save others the expenses I've incurred.

You may be wondering how my experiences may help you. Simple! A restaurant is a service oriented business. And, like any service oriented business you have direct interactions with your clientele, want repeat business, need referrals, and need to stay relevant to your guest/customer base: both current and potential. Like all service oriented businesses, you're not the only game in town and you want, need, and must, put a priority on positioning yourself as "THE" place to turn when the need arises. It is a great responsibility, perhaps a daunting task at first, but, oh, so very doable.

Here in *50 Mistakes Business Owners Make*, you'll find directly transferable, tailorable, and actionable ideas that can and will advance your business to a totally new place. Take the time to read through these lessons and learn from the mistakes I've made over the years and you'll be able to take a bit of shortcut to a higher more profitable road.

So, let's begin your journey now…

Acknowledgments

I'D LIKE TO EXPRESS deep gratitude to every single person who has given me the desire to achieve. Of course, my parents are first on this list. They instilled in me a very focused and determined work ethic. From a rather young age I was fascinated with the idea of buying something at a lower price and turning it around for sale at a profit. My parents definitely had me thinking business and working hard.

This book was also not possible without the mentors who greatly influenced me over the years. In great measure I owe the success of my business to them. Through them I learned to have an eye for perfection. While we all know nobody's perfect, I learned that the pursuit of it, rather the details of it makes for better results each time you do a thing.

I've talked about writing a book for years. This book is indeed a reality because of Carl Solomon. I have known Carl since the very first year Aroma Thyme was open. He was a great guest who understood our mission and personally lived it. We immediately connected. Later, we had the privilege of having Carl be part of our team for four years. Carl was our right hand man. Given his background in education, ability to present, and personal experiences, having him co-author this book was a natural fit.

I have the deepest gratitude and love for my wife, Jamie. She chose years ago to work by my side and run my dream restaurant with me. She and I have dedicated countless hours to the ins and outs of operating a business. Jamie is my number one mastermind and fan. Without her the reality of our success would not have been realized or look as good as it does now.

Marcus

I'D LIKE TO FIRST acknowledge my parents without whose consistent support, of the variety only parents, true friends, and spouses are allowed: I would not be the person I am today. Their encouragement for me to do what I wanted to do in life, coupled with loving parental reminders, wise advice, and of course the sometimes nagging to "get moving" on any one given thing I may have found myself stalled: is and always will be deeply cherished. To them I extend my deepest love and gratitude for always being there as parents and now also as the greatest of true friends.

I also wish to acknowledge my teachers, but in particular my English/writing teachers: who I lovingly quip, survived and graduated from *Our Sisters of the Bloody Knuckles School of Writing*. I hope this work meets with their approval for form and content.

Many I've known throughout my years of education and hiking the path of life-long leaner, exploring/seeking, have wanted to write a book. I am privileged to have this written work be a first for me as a collaborator and co-author. *50 Mistakes Business Owners Make* strikes at the very core of a personal and life-long mission for me: continuous/life-long education.

As a natural extension of this mission, I want to acknowledge Marcus and Jamie Guiliano. I first met Marcus and Jamie as a guest at their oasis of a restaurant, Aroma Thyme Bistro. Needing a change of direction for my life, I inquired about becoming part of their team. I greatly respected their mission and vision for their successful business. They are unique individuals who have created an environment in which both staff and guests have the opportunity to learn, grow, and explore a rather wide range of food, beverage and business related ideas and practices. They're essentially an open book to just about anyone who takes the time to inquire.

This work is truly a natural extension of who I am and who they are. It has been an honor and privilege to share this part of my life-long learning hike with Marcus by co-authoring this book. We hope it helps you further your journey of life-long learning and success.

Carl

Introduction

YOU HAVE A DEEP love for cooking and have since you worked alongside your grandmother. You've cooked something nearly every day since. You've perfected your craft and now you want to open a restaurant. It is not necessarily as simple as getting a piece of property and going for it. You are going to be opening a business which takes a whole set of skills and knowledge that don't necessarily come naturally. It is vital you consider all that goes into running a successful business. Unless you have a well written plan and/or years of experience, you are very likely going to make a tremendous number of costly mistakes. Even with a well written plan and careful follow-through you're going to make mistakes. There is a mountain of truth contained in the following words, "Those who fail to plan, plan to fail." Perhaps the greatest wisdom can be gleaned from those who have gone successfully before you and planning will help you minimize the cost of your mistakes while maximizing your profits along the way. Even those with years of successful experience fail when they stop the practice of planning. Don't let previous success become complacency and an environment for breeding failure.

Scott Shane, writing for *Small Business Trends* (*www.smallbiztrends.com*), plotted the five year survival rates for businesses in various sectors taking these data from Census Bureau's Business Dynamic Statistics (*http://www.census.gov/ces/dataproducts/bds/data_firm.html*). The sectors and their survival rates were as follows: mining (51.3%);

manufacturing (48.4%); services (47.6%) wholesale and agriculture (47.4%); retail (41.1%); finance, insurance, and real estate (39.6%); transportation, communications and utilities (39.4%); construction (36.4%). Given these data one might be discouraged from ever opening a business of any kind.

More to the point of this writing; you are going into the restaurant business and these statistics are in line with the foregoing. In an article for *Bloomberg Business Week* in 2007, Kerry Miller, cited research conducted by H.G. Parsa on restaurant failure rates, ultimately debunking the 90% failure rate. Parsa revealed that approximately 25% of restaurants close or change ownership within the first year of business. Over a three year span, that number becomes 60%. (http://www.businessweek.com/stories/2007-04-16/the-restaurant-failure-mythbusinessweek-business-news-stock-market-and-financial-advice).

While the urban legend of 90% failure rate for restaurants is bad enough to make anyone stop and reconsider opening a restaurant, in my opinion a 60% failure rate is just as bad. It is, however highly informative. As mentioned above, others have gone before you and you are likely to know at least one other successful restaurant owner. You needn't reinvent the wheel and make all of the same freshman mistakes of those who have failed. You will make your own mistakes. By looking to the success of others you can significantly minimize the risk of having to close your doors after the first year or the third.

My philosophy of restaurant ownership has evolved during the nearly fourteen years I've been an owner/operator. Perhaps the biggest change in my perspective now is operating my restaurant from the perspective of providing jobs for others: not me. If you can grasp this concept now, you may invariably find yourself in a vastly different place much sooner than you expected or even hoped to. You need to recognize ultimately the scope of your influence is much broader, and you need to begin to think this way starting now.

You are opening a business and will be providing jobs for others. Think in terms of training them so well you find yourself in the position of being a consultant for your own business. Your job is to empower staff, train them and use them for their skills.

I'm not saying you become superfluous to your business: to the contrary. There is a balance you're striving for that will afford you a bit of freedom down the road. A freedom which you have yet to either consider or fully embrace is possible and real. The Chinese proverb, "The journey of a thousand steps begins with the first", is well applied here. It is my intention to provide you with an outline of a few, well more than a few, common mistakes and overlooked details that not only cause restaurants to fail, but also keep them from growing when they are not intentionally/purposefully addressed. I have been down the road of making many of these mistakes and have learned, costly as it may have been, how not to keep on making them. In *50 Mistakes Business Owners Make*, I set about laying some of the foundation for you. Hiring a coach to help you maneuver the ins and outs of the finer points is definitely something you need to consider as well.

Let's begin…

There are several questions you need to ask yourself before you even begin looking for a property in which to invest. The following are in no particular order, but are meant to evoke deep consideration as your success will be contingent upon the depth of your knowledge, understanding, and follow-through.

An important note to highlight here before going any further is I will not be referring to "customers" or "clients" in this work. Experience has taught me while the words "customer" and "client" may be true and accurate, these do not impart the appropriate frame of reference for the desired outcome in my restaurant. We, (my staff and I), refer to our patrons as guests. We want each and every person who comes through the doors of our restaurant to feel at home, well cared for, special, and part of a greater whole. With just about all service businesses you want your clientele to be made to feel welcomed and cared for. It is the expressed mission of Aroma Thyme Bistro to truly attend to the complete dining and educational experience of our guests and engender a feeling of family

Do you know…?

- What you're looking for in staff?
- How to supervise your staff?
- How to conduct continuously progressive training for your staff?
- How to order your stock/supplies so these are consistently and properly rotated (where applicable)?

- How to cost and spec each dish and drink on your menu?
- How to run inventory for food cost?
- How to create a target inventory based on your sales mix?
- How to manage labor costs (your single largest expense)?
- How to keep and maintain all of the necessary equipment?
- How to not get taken by your vendors and get the best possible quality for the price?
- About having a defined customer relations policy?
- About customer retention, incentive and data collection?
- How to negotiate vendor contracts and not get ripped off by poorly negotiating?
- How to set up systems and utilize the systems to manage staff?
- How to work on your business rather than in your business?

While there are other items that can be included in the above list, the foregoing are excellent examples of what is required as a daily review for success in your business.

If you're feeling overwhelmed at this point, take a deep breath. A good deal of what you need to attend to may already be within your experience base. In order to assist you in not feeling overwhelmed, I'm going to guide you through reframing your thinking/perspective. Let's take the first step.

I.   Guest Relations

Mistake #1:   You're not collecting guest data.

Selling your cookies

LET'S SAY YOU ARE beginning to sell cookies because someone (friends/family) said you have real talent and your cookies taste awesome. One day you decide to bake twelve dozen cookies and set up a stand. It takes you eight hours to sell out of all the cookies. The second time you go out and sell another twelve dozen and it takes the same eight hours. During this second experience you notice you have repeat customers (your guests) and you collect some basic contact information so you can inform your returning guests the next time you'll be baking. After gathering their information you send out thank you notes for the repeat purchase. You also inquire if there is some other kind of cookie you might bake.

Before you even bake the third time you inform your guests you're baking again and you're adding a new cookie. During this process you obtain confirmed orders and are essentially able to sell out in advance. Be proud of your efforts. You've made your dough (yes, pun intended) and didn't have to take the eight hours to do it. As you continue to grow your baking business, you continue to collect contact information to keep your guests apprised of your location, current offerings, and upcoming events.

Information to collect: name, address, email address, phone number, birthday and/or anniversary, permission to utilize comments/feedback, disclosure of what you will do with the information you've gathered, and a guarantee you are not going to sell their names or personal information.

Methods of collection: Gold fish bowl, comment cards (do not hijack names), surveys, contests. Getting your guests to sign up is of course critical to creating a database. When and how they sign up is first and foremost. The most obvious being when they're sitting in your establishment. The next would be at fairs, tastings, chamber of commerce mixers, and of course on your website. Be creative, any time you are in front of people is a potential opportunity to be engaged. Be prepared. Make certain you are getting your customers' names and contact information with their permission so they will be comfortable with you contacting them and providing them with information.

Mistake #2:   You don't use in-house comment cards.

THE UTILIZATION OF IN-HOUSE comment cards has become more common, though in our opinion still not used nearly enough. And, when these are used there is insufficient follow-up on the part of the business owner. My wife and I travel a good deal and eat out frequently. We've filled out such cards, both positive and negative and very often have not ever received any sort of follow-up. Once we left a respectful complaint/constructive criticism, were responded to by the chef/owner, were told we'd receive a discount for a return trip and it was never sent. This is NOT a good business practice. Not only are we not likely to ever to return to this particular establishment, we're also not going to recommend anyone going there.

Comment cards are used for essentially two basic purposes: to gather feedback for what you're doing right and for what you're not doing right. Frankly, you're in a service oriented business and your success is contingent upon consistently excellent service. The nature of this beast requires you to obtain both sides of the story in order to be healthy. Ultimately, and especially for the positive and glowing feedback we're all looking for, you want to be able to reach out to your guest and request the use of his/her positive comments for publication. Conversely, you also must reach out to the guest with a negative experience and respond to it appropriately (more on this later).

I've used positive comments on our menu, website, Facebook and Twitter publications. In order to use these comments you must have permission from the guest, especially when it comes to posting the guest's name. Remember, you're not going to give up your guest's privacy. It is a very powerful thing to be able to post both first and last name in a positive comment for marketing. You've gotten someone who is willing to put their "name" on the line for your business. This becomes an unpaid endorsement from a community member and it is a huge validation to the claim you have the best steak in town, or you make the best martini, or the service is outstanding, etc....

There are means by which you can entice people to fill out your comment cards. At Aroma Thyme Bistro we offer a drawing for something (gift certificate or free food) when a guest is willing to provide personal information table side and for filling out the comment card. Remember, you're making an investment in both your business and in your guests by doing this.

It is very important your comment cards are professionally printed and cut. Raggedy looking won't cut it. You want to make a meaningful and serious statement about your business. Have your cards printed on a heavy card stock and cut straight. This will make them easy to handle and file. In the end this will be a worthwhile expense.

Mistake #3:   Don't let your guests forget about you.

HOW MANY TIMES HAVE you heard from guests that they love your place and then you don't see them for months at a time? Maybe they come back a year from now or maybe they never come back, even after eating at your place a few times. The restaurant business is very competitive and you're not the only spot in town. If you are not doing your part keeping your guests' attention; you can't blame sporadic visits from your guests when they're lured away by another restaurant employing the strategies presented in this book.

Several industry surveys have noted your guests want to hear from their favorite restaurant about every twenty-one days. You can select the method of communication. However, it needs to be made abundantly clear the content of the communication is crucial. While a Facebook post, Tweet, or Instagram can be an excellent addition, these should not be the primary venues through which you communicate.

The type of communication I recommend and use most heavily is an email blast/newsletter. Perhaps the only thing better than an email is a personalized mailer/postcard. Even better still, is a handwritten personalized thank you card. Each of my staff has been tasked with writing at least one of these per shift. You've already gathered basic contact information about your guests and if you're not utilizing this resource you're shooting yourself in the foot. Other personalized mailers might include birthday, anniversary, or some other major event incentives. Sending these types of personalized mailers to your guests will quickly develop guest loyalty and remembrance that you're the place to go to celebrate special occasions.

In addition to the foregoing, you should also seriously consider a monthly or bi-monthly email newsletter. Sending these is a means of "talking" to your guest/potential returning "newbie" guest on a variety of topics related to your establishment. Once you've covered these then you might also create a Facebook, Twitter, blog, vlog, YouTube following. Find your niche and write, talk, etc....about your strength in the marketplace. You can use these communication platforms as a way of promoting "special" or "secret" offers as well, and by doing so you're creating a mystique around your restaurant where only the "in-the-know" are aware. There is a great deal of social power garnered for those selected as being part of the "in-group".

Content of emails and/or snail mailers is obviously up to you; however you must ensure you share from authority, accuracy, and truthfulness in all you write. Certainly doing so with a sense of humor is also important.

Mistake #4:   Your follow-up sucks.

BY NOW YOU ARE hopefully seeing a clear picture regarding how you really need to use your guests' comments, birthdays, and/other shared personal information to your advantage. The name of the game here is repeat business. How do you get your guests to come back? One of the most powerful methods for getting a new guest to return is the use of something called a bounce back offer. Your newly minted guest loved the experience at your place so much they provided you with all of their contact information, as well as some lovely words of praise. Not striking while this proverbial iron is hot is a serious, serious mistake. The very same is true with regard to obtaining referrals from your clientele. Someone is more apt to provide you with referrals during immediate interaction and when the mood is positive.

In addition to sending out a handwritten thank you card, send along a coupon for "x" percent off their next meal, a discount coupon for the entire meal, a free appetizer...something. The quicker this apparent "freebie" goes out the door, the quicker you'll see the newbie guest return. Not to belabor the point, but the whole notion of the "bounce back" is based upon the rapidity with which you send it out. For the visual learner think of a brand new basketball, when you drop it to the ground it springs back – bounces back immediately. If it didn't, you'd need to return it to the sporting goods store because it is defective.

At Aroma Thyme Bistro, my wife and I decided to develop a $10 off coupon, no strings attached with an expiration time of 60 days. Our average check is about $38/person, so the $10 offer is a nice sweet spot of value for our guests and for us. Any amount less just wouldn't work given the fact that most of our guests travel a minimum of 20-30 minutes to dine in our restaurant. Scaling the offer up or down will depend upon your average check among other factors. I don't suggest making the expiration date any longer than 60 days either. You want to create some sense of "urgency" in your loyal guests' returning in a shorter period of time without creating a sense of "desperation" to have to come back too soon.

I don't think I can emphasize this point enough: perception can go a very long way in service businesses. When guests perceive a good value and have a great experience they will invariably come back more often and bring new people along to share in the positive experience.

Ideas to consider depending upon your location and type of establishment might include creating a combo offer like purchasing one thing and getting something else or bringing in a guest and getting something for the two. There is no limit to the creativity you can put into this effort and create real value in the process.

While we live in a technologically oriented world, and I use it to the full, my preferred method of delivery for our bounce back offer is an oversized colored postcard that is snail mailed. It needs to be large enough to stand out in the mail and not get easily lost at home when they put it away. Make certain, as mentioned above there is a limit/expiration date on it. In fact, all of your offers need to have expiration dates. As mentioned, this strategy creates a sense of urgency. Make the date a realistic one. You're cultivating a regular guest, you don't want to waste your efforts with too short of a date, and you want to be respectful in the offer. Also, be willing to be flexible if someone comes back just after the offer expires. Remember, you created this to get guests in your restaurant, so honor the offer.

Mistake #5:   You don't have a loyalty program.

RECALL THE STATISTICS regarding restaurants mentioned at the beginning of this writing. You have a small hill to overcome in order to remain in business and become successful. You need to ensure you provide yourself every advantage over your local competition. Creating an air of exclusivity by having a members' club is one way of doing this. Every major hotel chain, airline, grocery store and major specialty chain has a members' program. They figured out a long time ago a loyalty program is an amazingly strong tool for positioning their business over others. Of course, having a strong product and/or service to begin with is very important. While it is becoming a bit more popular, most restaurants, let alone service businesses overall, are still relatively new to this concept. The ones already engaged in this aspect of running a business are generally extremely pleased with the results.

I use a program called Royalty Rewards© (www.RoyaltyRewards.com). Royalty Rewards is a comprehensive customer loyalty and database management system. Conveniently built into this service are: bounce back offers, tiered discounts, guests' satisfaction surveys, and communication to guests. For us, there is POS integration and database generation. The power of the data gathering from this tool alone cannot be overstated. The investment in this service is well worth the cost. I can track guest preferences (both food and beverage), amount of money spent per guest per quarter and/or per annum. Tracking individual guest spending allows me to tailor promotional tiers to fit our needs, as well as, recognize guests individually with rewards if/when I chose. While it does take time to develop to this level of data gathering and usage, you are not in this to be a proverbial flash in the pan, but you are in this to make money and be successful over the long haul. There is NO better time to start than NOW. The beauty is that you needn't go this route alone. It is easy to find someone who can show the ropes and guide you through the process.

Remember you are intentionally nurturing guest loyalty in order to create a faithful and devoted following for your business. This is a process that takes time and needs to happen. Never forget, you're not the only show in town and patrons, even the steady ones, are generally a fickle bunch. It won't take much by way of a bad experience in turning off a new or returning guest in remaining loyal to your business. Even more so, guests will abandon you if they stop feeling like they're no longer getting a good value. Again, never forget value is not just measured monetarily.

Mistake #6: You don't keep or appropriately use your database.

ONCE YOU HAVE ALL this collected data and history/profile of your guests' spending you need to be able to disaggregate and analyze what you have. When reviewing your data you might notice immediately you have certain times during the year where you have a significant lull in sales versus a time when your business is slammed nearly every night of the week. This might be the first place you look to create promotions to enhance sales so you have a fuller dining room and elevated sales year round. You might notice your guests' spending clearly lays out into one, two, or three categories of low, mid, and high dollar amounts spent. If your POS is set up to track your food sales, resulting in something you use as inventory management you should be able to analyze what items move and what items do not move.

Do you see the picture being developed here? Data, data, data are the key to clearly understanding how your restaurant/business operates. These data inform you of how you're doing, what you're doing, and in the case of honest customer feedback, even why you're doing what you're doing. In each of the data sets presented here, a savvy business owner will make informed and intelligent choices on how to change, modify, and enhance the operational aspects of his/her restaurant. I keep making this next point in order to keep you from feeling overwhelmed: You do not have to go this alone, others have done this before you. Seek guidance when you need it.

Mistake #7:   How to get a guest to spend $5K? You don't know the value of a "lifetime" guest.

Y OU'VE NOTICED REGULARS IN your restaurant. You see some people will order high ticket items when they come in once a month. You have a person who comes in for happy hour every week and orders wings or a burger. It's a smaller transaction, but your happy hour guest is as consistent as clockwork. You have some who just come in for beer. In fact, you have all types of spenders who have become regulars in your establishment. You have an idea of what your check average is. However, you have no idea who your best guests are as far as overall dollars spent individually, and frankly you should.

In fact you should know the lifetime value of each guest in your database. If you don't you are missing a key component to managing your guests. I have discovered that the once a week guy for a beer, wings and/or maybe a burger is among our top tier spenders by year's end. Let that sink in for a moment. Your staff might think, "Oh, here comes the big spender!" (Read that with sarcasm.) As it is said, "Don't despise small beginnings." It shocks most restaurateurs when they run a purchase history and do a comparison. Your "big spender" is contributing significantly to keeping you in business. Remember what I said earlier; you're developing a loyal following of guests. It matters not whether they spend $15 per visit and come in 25 times per year or they come in one or two times per year and spend $150 per visit. Invariably you're going to have both types of guests regardless.

My wife and I have discovered our "lifetime" five year guest value is around $6800/guest. How many of these would you like to cultivate, in addition to going after first timers? These "lifetime" guests are your bread and butter, so to speak. Certainly, you can't do anything about this if you haven't identified who these "life timers" are.

As I mentioned we reward our guests using a tiered approach based upon the amount of money each guest spends through the course of the year. This definitely contributes significantly to creating our "lifetime" guests. We reward each level with a series of discounts, mailed to their home. We also target times of the year with various promotions in order to get more traffic through our restaurant. Yes, like many of you already in business and those of you starting out, we're not busy every day of the year. Even we experience slower times.

Using a tiered rewards allocation we reward our most frequent and/or higher spending guests with higher and/or more frequent discounts. Certainly I'm not suggesting you give away the farm. Managing this type of discount structure is readily accomplished through the Royalty Rewards© Program. The core of this service is data collection. The metrics gained from your guests' visits readily turns into a clear understanding of who is spending what, and when they are coming into your restaurant. This is essentially no different than a frequent flyer program; in this case, you'll be creating a frequent eater program.

With regard to a tiered approach, we have structured a three level approach to spending simply by analyzing the metrics generated by the Royalty Rewards© Program. I developed the parameters for how the discount rewards are sent, these preferences are loaded into the loyalty program and our guests are sent the discounts as they hit the respective tiers.

In addition to rewarding any guest who elects to sign up and participate in the Royalty Rewards© Program, my wife and I have created a special event to acknowledge those guests who fall into our highest spending tier. We call this the "Top 50". Each year we invite these guests for a day of appreciation. Included in this event is also a category of those guests who represent the "Top 50 Lifetime" members.

Recently we had three of these events (two to honor the "Top 50") so it really was the top 100, and one to honor the Top 50 lifetime. Recall I said to target a time of year for certain promotions and events when you know you're going to be a bit slower. We hold this event during mid-late January, which is historically the slowest time of the year for us. It should be obvious what this "give-to-get" event affords us. We have guests in the restaurant, we turn over food/stock, and our guests invariably order more than what is provided (though we do put up a very nice spread), our staff is engaged, and we've honored our guests.

The other perhaps, not-so obvious element of this event is our honored guests feel as though they're "insiders" and "part of the in crowd." The feeling of being part of a community is a powerful attraction and will significantly contribute to your guests' loyalty, the free advertising of positive word of mouth, and of course, provide substantially to your bottom line.

Mistake #8:   You don't understand the value of
                    paying to get new guests.

I T SHOULD BE STRIKINGLY apparent by now the value of taking the time to learn who your guests are. What are you willing to spend to get more of those who are lifetime oriented? I can sense you bristling right now at this thought. You're probably thinking spending $250 is not what you'd prefer doing, but would rather see $250 being spent by a guest at this moment. Most restaurants will spend $500 or more on print advertising (newspaper, magazines, etc....). Worse still, whatever guests do end up coming into their restaurant as a result of this traditional advertising expenditure, the business owner doesn't collect any data that can more readily guarantee a positive financial return. Happily, you're not going to be one of those one of those because by this time you've already made the necessary changes.

The bottom line: I regularly invest $250 to get back $5000+ over the next five years. I'm not saying this is what you're going to have to spend every time to acquire a new top quest, but I am suggesting you need to make a clear, purposeful, and targeted investment in obtaining new guests. Targeting your advertising and the venue in which you choose to do so is important. One of the ways in which you can refine this aspect of your business' success is to ask your current guests to bring in someone new. You can reward your current guest with some sort of gift card/discount for a future visit if they oblige. Explain to these top guests you want to find more great guests like themselves.

I don't invest in any "traditional" advertising at all. I want you to think beyond traditional radio and print advertisements. The above paragraph is one way of non-traditional advertising and it provides you with nearly guaranteed results and those you don't pay for unless it delivers. Other ways you can advertise is to give away $25 gift cards at mixers, professional, and/or chamber of commerce events. You might invest in purchasing a list of names for your locale and target the birthdays on the list or the zip codes in your area. Remember, special events are a large reason people go out to eat. You might entice newbies with a $10 off the purchase of two entrees. With these types of discounts you're enticing new guests, looking to provide some value, and not break the bank. Experience has demonstrated to me that these types of communications are best done via hard copy: so send an oversized postcard.

Big caveat here: Don't do any of this without informing your staff. Make certain they understand what to be on the lookout for and the details of the promotion. It speaks volumes when staff is able to respond quickly and knowledgably.

Mistake #9:   You don't know how to use social media to your advantage.

IT'S HARD TO BELIEVE how a teenager can change your life and a global culture so quickly and so dramatically. That's right. The internet is still a teenager. The exponential development of the "instant" technologies utilizing the internet has caused our marketing approaches to expand and change.

I know there are a lot of restaurants that have been in business 30+ years. Respectfully, they're generally the "old timers" of the industry and these dinosaurs aren't going to be around much longer. Many of these owners don't think they need social media. Depending upon the location of such restaurants, their guest roster may be declining because their aging patrons are thinning out. True we have a longer lived population today, but we don't succeed in this business resting upon our laurels. Changing times require exploring new ways of getting new guests through our doors to keep our restaurants vibrant and relevant.

Social media can be a true double edged sword. In the hands of the wrong person it can be damaging to the point of no return. In the right hands, properly, carefully, and strategically used it can be a huge boon to your business with a minimal investment of finances and time.

Social media can be used for public relations and marketing promotions of various kinds. It can be used for reputation management and building a solid base of raving fans. It's another venue for building community around your business which can lead to garnering both loyal and new clientele.

So, what is social media? The following definition is cited from *www.whatis.techtarget.com.*

Social media is the collective of online communications channels dedicated to community-based input, interaction, content-sharing and collaboration. Websites and applications dedicated to forums, microblogging, social networking, social bookmarking, social curation, and wikis are among the different types of social media.

Some prominent examples of social media include:

- Facebook is a popular free social networking website that allows registered users to create profiles, upload photos, send messages and keep in touch with friends, family and colleagues. According to statistics from the Nielsen Group, Internet users within the United States spend more time on Facebook than any other website.

- Twitter is a free microblogging service that allows registered members to broadcast short posts called tweets. Twitter members can broadcast tweets and follow other users' tweets by using multiple platforms and devices.

- Wikipedia is a free, open content online encyclopedia created through the collaborative effort of a community of users known as Wikipedians. Anyone registered on the site can create an article for publication; registration is not required to edit articles. Wikipedia was founded in January of 2001.

- LinkedIn is a social networking site designed specifically for the business community. The goal of the site is to allow registered members to establish and document networks of people they know and trust professionally.

- Instagram is a photograph, video content sharing site.

- Reddit is a social news website and forum where stories are socially curated and promoted by site members. The site is composed of hundreds of sub-communities, known as "subreddits." Each subreddit has a specific topic such as technology, politics or music. Reddit site members, also known as, "redditors," submit content which is then voted upon by other members. The goal is to send well-regarded stories to the top of the site's main thread page.

- Pinterest is a social curating website for sharing and categorizing images found online. Pinterest requires brief descriptions but the main focus of the site is visual. Clicking on an image will take you to the original source, so, for example, if you click on a picture of a pair of shoes, you might be taken to a site where you can purchase them. An image of blueberry pancakes might take you to the recipe; a picture of a whimsical birdhouse might take you to the instructions.

- And, any others that have come and gone since writing this book.

Keep in mind these are only the current scope of the more popular platforms. A new technology or potential media outlet could readily appear overnight. Staying current can be an important thing. For instance, there is a wearable device called the *Cicret Bracelet* which is making the rounds on the internet as a preview of what is coming.

The funny thing is that lots of businesses are on social media platforms, but aren't active. I know of a local business owner bragging about her 200 likes on her business page. When asked how she was communicating to her 200 likes, she looked at me blankly. She had no clue of the potential benefit to her business. She had yet to post anything herself, acknowledge or further market her business. I quickly realized this was not an isolated example. There are many more businesses that have failed up to this point to leverage the powerful marketing tool literally at their fingertips.

Simply signing up on Facebook or Twitter is nothing more than a perfunctory first step. You have to actively engage and pursue your newly formed connections with conversation, and yes, with some shameless self-promotion. A caution needs to be put forward here: this all must be balanced with purposeful content as well. Simply engaging in empty conversation is as bad as only promoting your business and products. People will see right through this.

Target your involvement by asking questions. For instance, if you own a beer bar, ask on a Monday what your subscribers/followers drank over the weekend and if anything was a standout or a dud. Since people love to talk, you'll get some great answers and invariably someone will say how much they enjoyed coming to your place and the great beer they tried that everyone else should try.

As you get your social on, remember all of the activity and communications put in these venues is public and will impact your business. Keep your communications professional, respectful, and thoughtful. Use this tool to both market and create active community that will result in becoming real bodies/traffic in your brick and mortar business.

II.   Business Operations

Mistake #10:   You don't have a website or don't maintain the one you have.

IF YOU DON'T HAVE a website today, you're missing out on the huge potential of near immediate gratification. Interestingly, many tweens, teens, and twenty somethings have their own websites, while a good number of businesses out there don't have a website at all. Worse than not having a website in the current business environment is having one that is very badly done or not representative of whom they are or what they do. It must cultivate more interest and revenue. There are excellent reasons for putting the effort into building a website and then maintaining it. In the spirit of David Letterman's famous *Top Ten Reasons…*, the following ten excellent reasons for having a website were taken from:

(http://www.localwebsitedesign.com/top-10-reasons-to-have-a-good-website/).

10.   You have more credibility by having an Internet presence in today's age. A business without a phone number or a physical address can seem shady. It's slowly becoming accepted that a business must also have a website and an email address. How many times have you looked for information about a company, and was left in the dark?

9.   Your website is always on call. Your website works for you 24-7 with no labor costs. Your website markets your business for you while you sleep. What more could you ask for? Hiring a 24 hour staff to answer the phone would cost thousands more a year, and be much less effective. Leaving a contact form on your site, allows potential customers to reach you at their convenience, and for you to get back to them at yours.

8.   Potential customers can find your business online, any time, on any device. Not too long ago, customers looking for your product or service would have to look you up in the Yellow Pages. Today, potential business is lost to other companies with detailed and easy to use websites, with a pleasant, eye catching design.

7.   Marketing and social media on the Internet is much more cost effective than traditional marketing methods. Imagine free advertising that can reach globally? In today's online market, it's entirely possible, starting with a homepage website, which can be expanded to social media sites.

6.   You can see how many potential, or existing clients visit your page daily. Using analytical tools, you can find out exactly how many visitors come through, how long they spend on your website, and which pages they are reading. The same cannot be said for

print and TV spots. How often do you, yourself tune out when commercials are on? With the introduction of digital video recorders, Netflix, and the like, TV commercials are making their way into being a thing of the past.

5.   A website increases the geographic range of your business. If you are a small business, you rely on foot-traffic and referrals for your business. By leveraging the Internet, potential customers not within your immediate geographic area can also find your business. By utilizing online quoting and potential shops, you can expand your business as far as you choose.

4.   It's easy and cheap to change company information and marketing material on your website. You know how costly it can be to have to change product information or prices on all your catalogs, brochures, and marketing material. It's much cheaper, easier, and faster to change all this information online.

3.   Customer service can be handled on the website. How many times do you hear the same questions over and over from different customers? As with any business, most customers have the same set of questions and concerns. By having an FAQ (Frequently Asked Questions) online, you can reduce customer service costs and save yourself time and money. You can provide more information than cannot be covered on a business card or flyer.

2.   A website conveniences your customer. Your customer can peruse your website at their own leisure. There's no pressure to buy nor do they have to drive over to your place of business to find out about your offering.

1.   A website address is easier to remember than a phone number.

Okay, so you're getting a hundred, two hundred, maybe more, views a day on your website. You might have some impressive web traffic for being a small business. Ponder these questions.

- Are these people staying and reading your site?
- Does your website turn these visitors into guests/clientele (revenue for your business)?
- How have you left a lasting impression that motivated a return visit and not forget about you?
- Do you know who is visiting?

Mistake #11: Gee, that empty restaurant sure looks like fun!

AMONG THE WORST MISTAKES you can make in advertising your restaurant is publishing pictures of an empty restaurant. Think about what the unspoken implications are of doing this. It is very easy to rectify this mistake as well. Most people, whether they can articulate this or not, go to and/or return to a restaurant because of an emotional connection. Perhaps the simplest connection to identify is the restaurant has a good vibe. Others include going to a particular place because they like the staff, the food is outstanding, or the wine and beer selection is superb. Do you want to go to a restaurant that is empty or go to one that is a happening place?

A restaurant pictured with empty chairs does not convey the place is happening, but rather devoid of emotion and energy. When you post pictures on your website they need to evoke some emotional response or memory. It's really that plain and simple.

There is one big however…make sure you have permission from the guests you photograph before publishing them for commercial use. This is critical. In fact we suggest going as a far as creating a press release permission statement that you have the guest sign so you can use his/her image. This also applies to your staff. When we hire a new person, as part of the hiring process, there is a press/appearance release form. We don't make this mandatory, but it covers us and the staff member. It saves you from the potential of legal action.

Pictures are worth more than words and by picturing your business to the world in a positive and warm manner, you're telling a story that will garner excellent outcomes.

Mistake #12:   You don't grow your sales.

W E ALL HOPE TO grow our business from year-to-year. In fact those who have their act together make a budget that projects increased sales. However, more often than not business owners have no idea how they're going to intentionally make an increase happen.

Part of intentional sales increase is to know who your most profitable guests are. You need to know as much about them as possible so you can create a profile, which you will in turn use to target this particular segment of your local population through the various forms of advertising and marketing you conduct. There are business services that can aid you in this process.

From our experience, we know birthdays are among our greatest promotional sales and this can very likely be yours as well. Given that this is a significant source of revenue through repeat sales, we take the necessary steps to find out each guests' birthday and we go one step further. We send a "half-birthday" incentive to our guests and do this exclusively through our involvement with Royalty Rewards© Program. Recall I stated earlier the use of this program can be tailored for your specific purposes. The result is we not only get guests to utilize the birthday incentive they receive, but six months prior to their birthday they receive an additional incentive to return to our restaurant.

Another possibility is the development of a catering option. We have ventured down this road with significant success. You might target your local business district and offer holiday parties either in office or in the restaurant. Certainly weddings (depending upon the size of your facilities) or off site catering might work for you. Perhaps you might develop a niche market locally for a particular catering need: for instance, networking with non-profit organizations needing to raise funds. Since many organizations look for donations, you can facilitate an arrangement for the non-profit organization "earning" your donation in exchange for free advertising for the services rendered to them. Additionally, you might strike up some sort of business relationship with the local funeral homes. Just remember not to compromise your mission or the quality of your food in the process. Catering can be a risky venture but doing it superbly can easily make for new lifetime guests as a result.

Developing your presence in the catering market can be as simple as being the provider for an event hosted by a couple of your regular guests, or by attending a bridal/wedding trade show, flower show, local business/trade convention, or whatever is part of the fabric of your locale. If you go down this road, make certain you do it well and make certain you create a spin off website dedicated to this purpose. Like your main business, you need to develop a personality and life for it. Surprisingly, you'd be shocked to discover that while you're known for your excellent fare your guests may not even consider you for a catering gig unless you put it out there. Both implied and stated has been the notion of "intention" and for very good reason. Unless you "intend" to do a thing and purpose to let others know, you won't grow your sales.

It can't be overstated you need to plan, test, and let others know what you are doing. The only things that grow well in the dark are mushrooms. Your business requires a light shining on what you do well and a light shining on what you're branching out to develop new. Make sure you have someone with whom you can bounce your ideas off of and with whom you can be coached. Success happens when you plan and plan well.

Mistake #13:   You don't avail yourself of those who've gone before you. The highest form of flattery is...

IMITATION. This is how we learned to walk, talk, eat, speak. Why don't we do this same sort of thing when we're learning how to be successful? I hear from so many business owners it's hard for them to be creative in their marketing approach. I hate to break the news to you, but many, many successful businesses really aren't all that creative. These folks are successful because they are keen observers and listeners of what other restaurants do and then formulate the demonstrated success into something that will work for them. It's just like cooking. Everything that works has already been done. There's a reason why you don't smoke an $18/pound lobster tail. It's because it was done years ago and they realized it wasn't good.

The same thing holds true for marketing. Go to other restaurants and do lots of research. Ask questions of the servers and the manager. Ask the owner if he/she is available. You'd be surprised to find out lots of business owners are willing to share what has worked and what has not worked: though we wouldn't necessarily suggest doing this sort of inquiry within the business community in which you operate. When you travel for business or when you're on vacation, inquire when you go out to eat. We've found managers/owners will open up to you if you identify yourself.

My wife and I are involved with a Mastermind group that meets a couple of times a year. We frequently run ideas past this group when we meet and contact various members in between as the need arises. Not only have really excellent ideas been born out these conversations, but we've also saved a good deal of time, aggravation, and expense in talking through ideas that sounded good at first, but ultimately would have ended in disaster. Being part of this type of group has truly been very beneficial.

Why reinvent the wheel? My point here is imitation is the highest form of flattery and it can save you an incredible amount of time, energy, and effort. Take the best of what you've experienced from other establishments and figure out a way to deliver those experiences and make them uniquely yours. I've said this before: there are many who have gone before you and have been successful. You've experienced some of their success. By taking the best of their ideas and making them your own, you afford yourself the opportunity to stand out in the crowd.

Mistake #14:   You don't have a clue about how your vendors are charging you.

YOU ARE WASTING MONEY if you're not bidding out the goods you're buying. Don't confuse this with buying cheaper food. It's a matter of researching the product(s) you require and locating the vendors who have them. You need to then investigate the quality and the best price and service for the items delivered. You have to let your vendors know they have to work for your business. Price and service are the two factors you are after. If the price is great from one vendor but they never have the item in stock then it's not a good fit for the long term success of your restaurant. If you can't get the item you need to prepare something on your menu, then that clearly defeats the purpose of having the item on your menu in the first place. The point: you can't simply shop price alone.

Many restaurants I know have prime vendor contracts and/or they have a cost plus program. My father-in-law has been in the food service industry for 60 years. His family's business is a full line food distribution company operating in direct competition with the likes of US Foods and Sysco. I can honestly say I've learned the ins and outs of these prime vendor contracts and cost-plus scams. When a vendor offers you cost-plus 5% there is no way of knowing the real cost. More often than not they have a way of hiding the real price. Some terminology you'll need to know follows.

- **Sales Cost:** The minimum cost a vendor is willing to let an item go for. All of the company's costs have been factored in with a margin of profit. Then they'll sell it to you.
- **Landed Cost:** The cost of the item delivered to the door of the vendor. Included in this will generally be the vendor's expenses for warehousing and any related delivery costs of the item into their warehouse.
- **Sheltered Income:** This is generally a rebate given to the vendor, which they do not have to report to their clients. Sheltered income incentivizes the vendor to sell more of something and receive money in exchange. At the end of any given quarter or year the vendor who receives these rebates ends up paying less for the product and thereby makes more money in the end. This leaves their clients having paid more for something that could have been discounted.

Sheltered income is a rebate check food vendors get after the fact for buying "x" item over a certain time period. Don't think the vendor paying $1.00 for something is going to then distribute it for $1.05. You're a business person, there's no logic in that. The average markup is at least 20% to 25% in the food distribution industry. Produce distribution can see much higher markups still. Think about it. No food service company could survive on a 5% profit margin. Warehouse space, utility costs for constant refrigeration and freezer items, trucks, fuel, employees, etc....all come with significant costs.

Sheltered income and/or rebates can amount to thousands of dollars per year in revenue/savings for a distribution company.

You will never hear your distributor mention this perk they receive. Knowing this little pearl should keep you from signing a prime vendor or cost-plus contract.

The proper method for successfully engaging one or more distribution services for your restaurant is as follows. First you need to have a detailed inventory for all of your menu items to know what you're going to obtain through a distribution service. Once you've done this you will research several distributors and find out which of them has the item(s) you require to consistently present your menu to your guests. Provide each of the distributors with your list of items and then let them fight to win your business. Knowing that you're shopping for the best distributors to provide for your restaurant's needs should have them competing to win your business.

During this process make sure you negotiate multiple case purchases/discounts on the items you know you will move through quickly. Multiple case drops are beneficial for distributors because they too have to move the items they have in stock, otherwise they have money tied up in something, taking up room in their warehouse not making them money. Open conversation and negotiation with your vendor is ultimately a significant key to your success and it will be beneficial for them as well. They've gained another source of income that didn't exist before. So, tell your distributor you're willing to work with them and you're willing to negotiate to get the best prices possible.

You can go a step further. I attend multiple tradeshows per year. While there I speak to the brokers and sales reps of the products we purchase for the restaurant. I ask about what incentives or programs there are for them. You'd be surprised to learn how much financial support you can obtain this way. You're not necessarily representing your own restaurant when you serve a dish. Within the walls of your establishment lies a potentially larger billboard. Here's where you might get very creative and save some money. Tell the reps/brokers you're willing to name their brand on your menu. While not exactly "free advertising" for them you might gain better pricing in this manner because you are bringing vital product/brand name recognition to a wider audience that would otherwise be ignorant of the item.

Remember all the data you've been keeping? This is yet another place you can intelligently use it to your advantage. You should be able to tell the rep/broker that in the last three months or whatever span of time you've sold "x" portions of "x" product. You can then tell them you project the ability to sell "x" cases of said item. By using this particular technique I've been able to save 20%-30% on the cost of various products we use consistently.

If it's not apparent at this point, let me state it clearly. You MUST be able to monitor every single price for every single item coming through your door. You need a system that can track these costs for analysis both short and long term. Portion size, cost of the item on the menu, and your overall profit margins are hinged upon this data.

Don't go overboard when you see costs rising 2%. There are several paths you can take in adjusting your menu costs, but when you see an item trend upwards 10%-15%, then you will need to revisit your cost structure to best handle this and make the appropriate impact for your bottom line and guests' experience.

Experience is a wise guide but it often times comes at significant cost and heartache. For the sake of repetition, my experience dictates you do not sign exclusive vendor contracts/agreements. You know there are other players in this market and they know this too. When it comes to the finished product you serve to your guests, never, never cut corners in quality. Your reputation is on the line, as is the safety of your guests. Where and when you can negotiate a better price without compromising quality and safety: do so. All of your behind the scenes costs (propane, gas, oil, garbage, insurance, uniforms, etc....) can and should all be carefully researched, sourced, and negotiated for your benefit. Finding vendors who meet your needs for the "unseen" part of your business is foundational to your overall success and longevity.

Mistake #15:   You don't keep tabs on your business.

SO MUCH IMPORTANCE HAS been placed on a yearly check-up with your doctor. While this is a good means of keeping tabs on your overall health, it would be much better to have a check-up bi-annually, once per quarter, or even monthly. Your business is essentially no different in some respects, and requires tabs being kept on it.

Perhaps you've done your homework regarding the vendors you've engaged to provide the raw materials for your menu, but you've stopped there. Not keeping tabs on the rest of your business once the items come through the door is a serious mistake. In fact this is one of the stupidest mistakes many a business owner makes. Don't be lulled into thinking you're successful simply because you may have a positive balance in your checkbook. Yes, you WANT a positive balance in your checkbook, but that doesn't mean you're necessarily making the most you can. Knowing what each item on your menu costs to get it to the table is crucial to your overall success. However, this is only one of the things you need to know. You must also know what your labor costs are. Managing both your front of house and kitchen staff are significant factors in how much you either take home or leave behind as potential waste or loss. Further you must consider the cost of the beverages you offer to your guests.

Consider the following. You've reached a place where you want to hire another chef or a manager. Precious few of the people you may hire to fill a key position in your restaurant are going to have a clue about managing inventory and/or calculating costs down to the portion being served to your guests. Let me bang this drum loudly. This is your business and you must be the expert when it comes to managing your investment. It also means that while you may hire someone who claims to know how to conduct an inventory and purchase items, you will invariably train each person in the key roles to do these tasks for your success, benefit, and to your specific needs. You may not be an expert at this point and you may even find being able to do these things is currently a weakness. I'm telling you for your own benefit you MUST make your weaknesses your strength or find someone who can coach you to become self-sufficient in the areas you are weak, so you can become the expert in your restaurant.

I spoke of return on investment (ROI) in your advertising budget. While these behind the scenes details are far from sexy or exciting, your ability to carefully and accurately maintain inventory, know the cost of items on your menu, cost of advertising, and how to train staff will see your positive checkbook balance go ever higher.

Early on in owning my own business I gained a much finer understanding of the numbers. I was able to save some $80K in expenses in one year alone. I had a positive balance in our checkbook the year before and I didn't think we were necessarily bleeding money. How profound and lasting an impact do you think it made on me when I discovered I could have saved close to $80K the year before? Who wouldn't want to take home another $160K? This is money that could have been used to reinvest in our restaurant and provide a bit more comfort for other things as well.

You must run your numbers regularly and in a timely manner. You need to set deadlines for yourself so you are always up-to-date. In my restaurant we run monthly comparatives from the year prior to the current year to see where sales are and to gauge how we're doing with our loyalty program. We keep close tabs on portion size and rotation of stock to ensure product waste is minimized to the greatest extent possible. I regularly meet with my kitchen staff to share this information. Sharing this information with my staff helps to make them feel empowered and included in the success of Aroma Thyme Bistro. If they don't know to begin with, they won't and can't have an opportunity to care. In many restaurants there are career servers and kitchen staff who depend upon your success. By informing your employees of what is going on, you are creating: a means by which to bring accountability to their jobs; a foundation for periodic evaluations of performance; the basis to potentially develop a real sense of "ownership" that goes beyond simple caring. Remember, you're in this to provide jobs for others, not one for you.

Let's think in somewhat more tangible terms at this point. If you can lower your overall costs by 1% annually, semi-annually, or quarterly you might make a significant improvement to your bottom line. I'm not from the school of thought that says lost revenue is a good write off on your taxes. Saving money you can re-invest in your business is a wise investment. If you're overall operating budget is $500K to $1M a year and you're able to save 1% annually, you'll be putting

$5,000-$10,000 per year back into your coffers to reinvest in your business or to set aside for something else you might require.

I've previously referred to having a coach guide you through this process. This is an area of business ownership that is often overlooked and is best done with someone who has the experience to guide you through the ins and outs of these processes.

Mistake #16:   You don't respond to the good.

I WILL GUIDE YOU through response time regarding negative feedback about your restaurant later. Here I will guide you through responding to the positive with respect to building your business because you should not take positive feedback for granted.

Remember you're using social media to build an online community that will build your brick and mortar business. By responding to the good, you are sending the message you are listening, willing, and unafraid of engaging with your guests. Your responses needn't be complicated or lengthy. I have a rather extensive listing of content posted to YouTube and I respond to all of the posted comments. This effort can take a great deal of time, so at a minimum I thank individuals for watching and commenting. The gesture of a simple "thank you" and mentioning something the viewer liked can go a long way. It shows you are human, engaged, and approachable. You can make very simple statements like: "Thanks for making the trip to come visit us."; "We're glad you enjoyed the jazz night, we like it as well"; or "We're glad you liked the house Malbec; we just found it and love it too."

Your online reviews go beyond Yelp and/or Trip Advisor. You'll find guest comments on Instagram, Twitter, Facebook, LinkedIn, and surveys. You will need to develop a system for managing all of the comments/feedback you receive so you can efficiently and effectively respond.

Yelp and Trip Advisor will send you a message when you are mentioned. This is the case with many of the others mentioned also. The use of Google Alerts can play a very important role here as well. Google Alerts is a free service. Simply register the name of your business to put an alert on it every time the name of your business is mentioned on the internet. Use these alerts to your advantage and don' be complacent about responding.

Mistake #17:   Your staff doesn't know how to ask questions.

WHEN YOU ASK BETTER questions you get better answers. This is something of a conundrum, which implies you have some knowledge of the subject in order to ask the better question to begin with. How many times have you been asked how everything was when you're out eating at a restaurant? And how often have you simply responded by saying everything was fine when in reality it wasn't? If the server asked, "Was your burger cooked to the perfect temperature"; then you might have responded, "Well it was a little under or overdone." You have to train your staff to ask the proper questions. It's that simple. When somebody did not eat all of their food your server needs to engage the guest with more pointed conversation. Some people are just light eaters and/or they're taking the food home for later. In many cases you can find out much more information by asking the right question(s) and well beyond the aspect of food. For instance, "Did your food arrive quickly enough?" "How was your martini?" Or, "Did you find a parking spot easily?"

Ask specific questions you will get specific answers. Certainly, don't stop once you've gotten the answers to the questions asked. Takes these back to formalized trainings for your staff. As a general rule we share every single written comment and review whether it's good or bad with our staff in a formalized staff workshop.

We conduct a post-meal email survey, in which we ask about the guest's experience and if they would recommend us. As an added incentive to get a response we offer "free" points to the guest's loyalty account. These points can push a guest to the next level of discount for a future visit.

How good are you at reading your guests? No, we're not talking about a psychic reading, but we are talking about reading faces, body language, and tone at the table. It's like reading the road when you're driving a car. If you've driven long enough in a wide variety of situations, then you hopefully have developed a true driver instinct through which you anticipate what the drivers around you will do based upon the road and traffic conditions.

It is no different when serving your guests. When you walk by a table after dropping off some part of your guests' meal, can you gauge their responses from the first bite? Can you then translate these experiences into staff development? Your staff has to feel as if they are the ones who need to keep your restaurant open by serving your guests as if the business is theirs. The higher the level of buy-in, responsibility, empowerment, call it what you will, your staff have in your business the higher the level of care, attention to detail, and the higher quality your guests' experiences will be. In short, your staff needs to "own" your guests' experiences. This means that every aspect of service needs to be beyond the personal standards of your servers and frankly, even beyond yours.

Comprehensively developing your staff is critical and this needs to happen in all areas of your restaurant. They must know your menu and other offerings (beverages, events, philosophy, founding story, etc....) like the back of their own hand. Unfortunately, you're going to have staff that has never seen the back of their own hand.

It is your business. Your success is in the hands of your service staff. They are the face of your business. Since you can't do it alone or be there all of the time, you must train your staff to read the guests, ask the questions, make suggestions, and know who to turn to for the solutions. If they can't do these things then you will not be a successful as you can be.

Mistake #18:   You don't answer the phone when it rings. Pick it up!

I T OUGHT TO BE clear to you by now, our society drastically changed with the advent of the internet and the cell phone. Most are now so connected that instant gratification or at least the perception of it has become something of a way of life. (We're not here to debate philosophical perspectives; we're simply highlighting an observation.) Take a look around and you'll find a good deal of the people you observe hang on their cell phones constantly looking at them, answering emails, responding to texts, or checking the latest updates to Twitter, Facebook, or some other social media or news alerts to which they're subscribed.

In short a great many have become addicted to their cell phones and technology and in large measure many have become ever more impatient. Even being conscious of, and knowing all of this, I often catch myself feeling terribly irritated and impatient when I call a business only to find no one is there to speak with and I have to leave a message. Does this sound familiar to you?

People want to be accommodated immediately. When someone calls your restaurant are they met with no answer at all, do they get an answering machine, or is someone there to answer the call?

This may or may not seem so obvious and it's quite simple. As much as possible, especially during times you're not physically in the restaurant: ANSWER THE PHONE WHEN IT RINGS.

Why am I spending time instructing on this aspect? It's very simple. Each time you don't answer the phone for your business it costs you money. The average phone call results in a request for reservations for a three top. If you're average guest spends between $20 and $40 per person then missing just one phone call could result in the loss of $60 to $120. If you're open six days per week, then your work year is 312 days. By missing one call per day you potentially miss out on some $18K per year in potential revenue, which is conservatively $345 per week based upon the numbers provided here.

Take a moment to digest (sadly yes, pun intended) the foregoing example. Let's use a more conservative example. You own and operate a small café with moderately priced fare. Your average check is $15 per person. You're open 6 days per week for 50 weeks each year, which amounts to 300 days of operation. You miss an average of 7 calls per week, which is a potential loss of 350 reservations per year. With an average check of $15 you've missed out on $5,250 of revenue. Can you really afford any loss at all?

Use the technology available to your advantage. We forward our restaurant phones to our cell phones in order to be in nearly constant contact with our business. Certainly nobody wants to feel like a slave to their business, but you are in this to make money and that requires you to have people in your restaurant. When we need a break, we have trusted staff who are very capable and knowledgeable about our business and who will field calls when we can't. A very important point is we have very little down or no answer time with our business. By being in touch and quick to respond we have busier nights and have minimized loss of revenue. Remember you're not the only venue in town, people do things last minute expecting immediate results. If it's perceived you're not open or not available the potential guest who called will very likely go somewhere else to eat.

Some last minor points. Always try to answer the phone within two to three rings. Make sure your entire front of house staff knows how to answer the phone and take reservations. Yes, there is knowledge and instruction required to be done for this to be successful. And, make very certain whoever answers the phone clearly represents your restaurant with a positive, open, professional and courteous attitude.

Mistake #19: You don't have a guarantee of satisfaction or your money back policy.

D O YOU HAVE THE confidence in yourself, your business acumen, and your product to guarantee what is going to end up in front of your guests is worth putting your money where your mouth is? (Okay, play with words here is important.) I feel there is a tremendous amount of power that comes along with having this kind of confidence. In the short run this may cost you money on some nights when following through on this plan. The situation surrounding your need to follow through with a money back guarantee may end up having you lose a guest, as they may be that upset. However, all in all, you will gain in the end. Sowing good will with your guests because of your level of confidence is paramount.

If you are unable to do as the foregoing suggests because you stress over every penny earned, look to nickel and dime your way through the business, you are doomed to fail. The adage the customer is always right (though there are times they're dead wrong) will cause you to still make good on your ability to offer the money back guarantee. Remember the best advertising is word of mouth and a bad situation made right and shared by your guest(s) to friends and family is very profound. I know from experience when I have heard of and/or have experienced a business owner make good on a situation: I have more respect for and am willing to give the establishment a second chance.

Very often I will share the story and say, the owner was on top of the situation and I want to go back.

A money back mentality is critical especially with the following. One of the worst things that can happen aside from having a brawl at your bar is perhaps, having someone throw up in your dining room uncontrollably. Not to be more graphic than necessary, but I'm talking about projectile vomiting here. It is more reasonable for a child to end up in this position given most adults know their bodies well enough to recognize the signs of this impending doom. If this were to happen in your restaurant on a busy night with guests witnessing the horror of this event, what would you do? While not apparent to your other guests, you know this is not a result of your food. In the instance I'm relating, the guest's response was the result of an allergic reaction because of said adult's very poor choice. He made absolutely no mention he was allergic to something commonly used in the dish he ordered.

I'm sad to admit the foregoing description of events happened in my restaurant. An adult proceeded to projectile vomit while sitting in his chair. After the first round he attempted to exit out the back door. He stumbled and bumped into other people eating. There were approximately 20 people in the dining room who witnessed this fiasco. It became one of those slow motion moments. We all kept hoping it was nothing more than a bad dream. Unfortunately it was no dream. The odor was terrible. It took four staff members with rags, mops, and a good deal of natural air freshener used at both ends of the dining room to take care of the problem.

By now you must be curious as to how we handled the situation. The answer is simple. We did everything we could to make as little fuss over the situation as possible. We moved as quickly, quietly, and unceremoniously as possible to clean up the mess. In addition to simply cleaning up the mess, I decided to comp the checks of the other 20 guests who witnessed the horror. This cost me a serious chunk of change that night. But, without question, everyone left praising and thanking us for how we handled the situation.

You need to reflect on this matter carefully. While the loss of revenue stung sharply in the short run, especially on the scale noted, I was able to turn the situation around and preserved at the very least, if not also gained a greater level deeper respect from the 20 guests who witnessed the awful event. I can happily share that all of these 20 guests have since returned many times and have brought new guests along as well.

You must be able to stand behind your business regardless of what goes on. This level of confidence will only serve you well in the end.

Mistake #20: **Cross Promoting: You don't leverage your confidence with other local businesses.**

ONCE UPON TIME THERE was an expression, "Does Macy's tell Gimbels?" Okay, so perhaps I'm dating myself a bit. You can glean the notion here. I'm referring to the competition and the implication of giving up trade secrets. I'm certainly not suggesting you give away all of what you do, but there is a demonstration of great confidence and power in being open to cross promoting.

Cross promotion is the intentional activity of local businesses supporting each other. Your local liquor store, the cleaners, a restaurant on the other side of town, even the local mechanic, are but a few examples of those you could cross promote. Do you have menus at the cleaners, the local tire place, or the local liquor store, the local car dealership? Do you even know who owns these places?

You have a place specializing in steak and seafood and you've got a fellow restaurateur five miles down the road specializing in Italian food. You know his product is good because you take your family there on occasion and you see him in your restaurant occasionally as well. The natural thing to do is sit down and discuss some mutual plan to promote each other's business.

This is the obvious way of moving forward. The not so obvious means of cross promotion comes when you expand your view of the local community and actively work with businesses outside of your expertise where you're not competing directly for customers.

An example of how this second means of cross promotion works might look like the following. As a restaurant owner you will frequently find you require tools and parts to fix various things that will inevitably break down. You have a hardware store in town and the owner of said establishment has come into your place several times. You sort of know who he/she is but have not necessarily had much conversation. You've made mistake number one that will need to be corrected immediately. Your place in the community is very important and knowing who the local business people are is critical to your success. At this point you should know how to fix this mistake.

Your local hardware store is very likely to sell a variety of items that could handily make for an excellent mutually beneficial venture. Co-sponsor a grill and steak giveaway and hold the event at the hardware store. Work out a deal with one of your food purveyors to supply steaks. Get the hardware store to work out a deal with their supplier on a particular model of grill. Assuming space is available, put the grill on display at both the restaurant and at the hardware store with the same signage announcing the giveaway.

Use all of your advertising outlets to promote the event (Twitter, Facebook, email newsletter, etc....) and the local hardware store should follow suit as well. Generally speaking in smaller towns, but also in larger communities you can readily get the local newspaper to take interest and do a piece and/or put some mention of it in the paper and on their website.

For a giveaway like the one described here, Memorial Day weekend or July 4th would be the perfect time to conduct such an event. Generally speaking you will need to begin promoting this event no later than six weeks prior to the giveaway. A well promoted event like this can generate hundreds, if not a thousand plus names.

Has the light bulb gone off in your head yet? Let me reiterate…A well promoted event can generate hundreds, if not a thousand plus names.

Both you and the hardware store now have a mailing list with which to contact and direct market. The name of the game for both of you is to get people into your businesses so that they spend money, so you make money.

You will only have one winner. They walk away with a shiny new grill and some steaks to cook. Both businesses walk away with an increased database of leads for potential new or returning customers/guests.

It will cost you absolutely nothing to go the next step. Send out an email to all who signed up telling them who the main prize winner was and that they have also won. Send everyone a $10 off coupon or a free appetizer coupon, free drink, dessert, whatever, but send something.

Strike while the iron is hot, your business name is fresh in everyone's head. You may get quite a few first time new guests out of this little venture. As for your partner in this, suggest a similar type of coupon for a discount or percent off a next purchase at the hardware store.

Mistake #21:   You don't have an opening line. You lose them at hello.

YOU CAN ONLY MAKE a first impression once. I'm certain you've heard this expression before and if you haven't then, take a minute or two to ponder the power of the statement. When you walk into a restaurant or any business you haven't been in before, the manner in which you're greeted can make or break a sale.

I've walked into many establishments and have experienced seriously lack luster greetings, if not outright disdain or the impression of it, by the employees or owner of the place. Generally speaking it doesn't bode well for future sales, let alone the potential to be walked out on. In point of fact, when I've been greeted this way, there have been several occasions where I simply turned around and walked out never to return.

So, I say again, "You can only make a first impression once." The guests who walk into your restaurant are there to spend money. They are doing you the favor, NOT the other way around. It is your responsibility, mission, obligation, raison d'être to greet each and every guest with the warmth and enthusiasm that says they're special and you want them to be there every night of the week.

If you don't do what is suggested here then you are running a very serious risk of not only losing the guest as a future one, but also losing out on all the new ones they'll go and talk to. Remember what the value is of each "lifetime" guest. The practical application here goes a bit beyond a simple hello, though that is of course the perfect place to start. Once you're past hello, pre-qualifying your guest before they sit down or on the way to the table is an excellent method of knowing how your staff can proceed. You/your staff may say, "Is this your first time dining with us or is this a return visit?" For a returning guest who may not be recognized by name, it's a good idea to thank them for returning. For first time guests you might thank them for choosing to dine with you.

Several things happen both consciously and unconsciously with the guest. You're establishing a level of confidence, acknowledgement, and warmth all at once. Once you've established which of the types of guests (first time, returning, or regular) you can further the conversation, education, orientation with them to continue to build upon your unique qualities, history/story, menu, philosophy, etc....

There's a reason we continue to repeat the line from the movie Jerry McGuire, "You had me at hello." You want your guests to be positively set up for what follows hello. If you need help coming up with your opening line(s) then seek out that Mastermind group and seek out the regular guests you trust. Find out how they would describe your business or how they advertise for you when they recommend your place to friends, family or business associates.

It is especially critical you train and monitor your staff to consistently follow through with your opening line(s). Allow them to develop their own flair, but ensure it remains respectful and within the "personality" of how you want your business portrayed.

Mistake #22:   You haven't turned the light on in the room yet...support locally.

EVERY CHAMBER OF COMMERCE and independent business owner touts supporting local. A number of years ago there was a bumper sticker affixed to many a car that read, "Think globally, act locally." We're told the American economy is fueled by supporting local businesses. Many business owners proudly display signs conveying they support the local infrastructure. At issue here is your guests may not experience a business that is operating in truth or in the spirit of local when visiting your establishment.

Perhaps the best way to highlight what I'm talking about here is the example of a chain restaurant. You could walk into a McDonald's and be supporting an independently owned, locally owned, or corporately owned store. I prefer, strive, and purpose to support locally and/or independently owned and operated businesses. A thriving community, especially the smaller ones exist in large measure, if not wholly on independently owned and operated establishments.

Most independently owned restaurants, regardless of community size do not engage the resources of their communities to supply the needs of the restaurant. Most restaurants purchase goods from large corporate purveyors. By engaging in this sort of business practice the locally owned, independent restaurant is only doing so much for the community in which they operate, and contributes instead to a larger corporate entity.

To be clear, I am all for being successful and making money. However, I intentionally seek to support, to the best of our ability, other locally owned and/or independently owned and operated vendors to supply our needs. Large corporations are not necessarily inherently evil. However, when most bars are stocked with items mass produced by companies that would happily destroy a small independent producer/competitor there is a serious issue. I do not choose to contribute to the coffers of these large corporations wherever I can.

It has taken a good deal of time, energy, and effort to, research, learn, and refine the things I offer at Aroma Thyme Bistro. From the bar, to the kitchen, to the table presentation I seek to support smaller companies with whom I can develop strong relationships and have a much better handle on the quality of the products being used at my restaurant. I want to represent the best of what is around us locally (farmed, raised, made) and source the best of what is available to us by way of craft produced items from around the country. The journey has not only been seriously instructive for me, but also for our guests who now also take pride in knowing what they are supporting by coming to do business with us. To say these efforts are both humbling and a source of great pride is an understatement.

If you can purchase local produce for some of your menu items, when it is appropriate of course, then I urge you to do so. While it may cost you more and take a bit from your bottom line, I think in the end you'll make more overall. By speaking to your guests and stating on your menu description, your broccoli or cauliflower came from XYZ Farm up the road from the restaurant, you'll not only be supporting your local economy, but you'll also be cross promoting. Your local farmer will, in all likelihood be very receptive to you having your menus and postcards on their farm stand. Seasonally, when they are busy, they'll also speak about your restaurant to those folks who are travelling through and you will gain new guests out of this arrangement.

In the end I sincerely believe it is better to consciously choose how you're going to supply your restaurant as opposed to taking the path of least resistance as many other restaurant owners do by simply getting all of their supplies from the local "one stop" type corporate purveyors. I acknowledge it will take more effort on your part, but it will be well worth it in the end for you, your guests, and the community in which you operate.

Mistake #23:   Horse trading is back. Do you know how to barter?

T HE EXPERTS SAY THE most expensive thing in your restaurant is an empty seat. I completely agree. If you have no guest traffic, then aside from not moving your food stock, you're also not generating future interest, word of mouth advertising, guest loyalty, or developing a reputation of any kind. You may as well just close the doors now and move onto something else. You've opened your restaurant to serve the guests that come through your door. What game plan do you have when things are slower or when you've just opened and are in the development state?

One creative means of getting people through your doors to sample your fine fare may be one of the least thought of and least used: bartering.

We all have needs in one way or another, tires for the car, perhaps some plumbing, electrical, or other repair requirements. If you've just opened the doors to a new restaurant and your contractor is already onto another project and you have some finish or refit needs, you'll need to engage someone to do the job. A picture should be forming at this point of where I'm going here.

You're a new business owner looking to create a reputation and traffic in your restaurant and you have some need. I suggest you engage another local business owner in some sort of horse trading. Offer a gift card for an equivalent amount for the item required for your business. The very worst thing that can happen is that you'll be turned down, though a smart business owner will give more serious consideration to this proposition.

If you're truly savvy about this and you've got all the details of how this works to your mutual benefit in your head then the pitch should go very smoothly. In the end both of your businesses will benefit: remember you can't buy word of mouth advertising, you have to earn it and this is an excellent way of doing it.

You're not going to barter with every business in town, but as a need arises, where it is appropriate, make this sort of effort and explore what is possible. Be creative in your thinking here, make the offer to barter a win-win, and be very clear about the expectations on both ends of the trade so there are no misunderstandings. Bartering can truly work out to be mutually beneficial.

Mistake #24:   You've forgotten how to play like a kid
                in a candy store. Go to a trade show or
                two.

YES, I AM SUGGESTING you get out of
your business and see what is going on in the "real
world". This is a field trip assignment not to
simply have a day off, but to explore and learn
what you can about what is going on related to your business.

While the essential elements of running a successful restaurant
have not necessarily changed in the last fifty years, some things
have changed dramatically. Being informed about what is going
on in today's society and how to respond to and communicate
those changes is quite important. The business your father
owned may be thriving today, but I would be very willing to
bet that in order for his business to have remained successful
there had to be some sort of course corrections and rethinks
along the way to stay relevant.

One of the ways in which I stay relevant and more fluid than
many other restaurants is by going to trade shows. It can easily
be agreed upon that technology has dramatically impacted our
lives in both profoundly positive and not so positive ways. The
increasing use of websites, social media, and advances in POS
systems, database management, and other service oriented
technology have contributed to making our lives a bit easier
and restaurants more successful by leveraging these tools.
Aside   from   operational   technologies,   there   are   also

advances/innovations in methods of food preparation, processing, and product offerings.

If you attend a trade show or two with an open and creative mind, you will not only see some new and cool stuff, you will find yourself being inspired as well. You may hit upon a new food trend a couple of months prior to the rest of your competition, or you may stumble across a piece of technology that can save you hours of time and some cash as well over the long run. I think one of the keys to your success is to strike the balance between what is tried and true for you and what is new and beneficial that can be implemented and/or changed with regularity.

Just one more thought here to drive the point home. Nearly every profession has some expectation for staying current/up-to-date with regard to knowledge in their field of endeavor. You need to have the same attitude and the same kind of curiosity. By exploring trade shows, addressing the various aspects of your business, you will be knowledgeable about a number of things your competition may not even know exists. Having an edge over your competition could mean the difference between an increase in your bank account or not having an increase.

Mistake #25: **Reading is definitely fundamental. Read those trade books and other related publications.**

I **THINK CONFUCIUS MAY** have said it best, *"No matter how busy you may think you are, you must find time for reading, or surrender yourself to self-chosen ignorance."* In the previous mistake I talked about getting out and going to trade shows. While there is nothing like being there, live and in person, the next best thing would be to read trade journals, magazines and books. There are also a few good email newsletters that can keep you abreast of what is happening in the world of the restaurateur.

It's not enough for you to simply read through these publications or to simply go to the shows themselves. Au contraire mon ami…You must be actively reading and develop being self-reflective during this process of exploration and learning. While pouring over the various trade publications/magazines you will discover trends in food, beverages, equipment, hardware, technology and sometimes and very importantly new laws.

As already stated you must read through these publications with the goal of becoming self-reflective and self-critical. No one else is in the room with you so honesty shouldn't be an issue. I stress this point because in being nakedly honest and candid with yourself about where your shortcoming/failings/weaknesses are will only fuel a positive direction for your business.

Investing this time as a research project can keep you far ahead of other business owners and at some point could inspire you to either create or adopt something that will put you far ahead of your competition long before they even get a glimpse of the coming trend.

I offer a word of caution. Don't find yourself running after every trend just because it is a trend. You need to weigh your mission/vision and "personality" and judge whether what you've seen is a worthwhile investment. Simply and obviously, if you're a steak house, you're not going to invest in a really cool new sushi presentation case even if it's going to look totally awesome in your dining room.

I really can't emphasize this enough…if you want to succeed beyond the average, knowledge is your key. Whether it be a new trend or law, if you stay cloistered in your establishment then you're not going to progress. It takes intentional effort to be the success you want to be.

Mistake #26:   You don't have the confidence to talk to your competition.

A S MENTIONED PREVIOUSLY MY wife and I are members of a Mastermind group and have been since 2007. Membership has both its costs and rewards. At the time of this writing we invest about $10,000 per year to maintain a membership in this particular Mastermind group and we only meet three times per year. This is perhaps the single best investment of our time, energy, and money we make every year. Between various presentations, breakout sessions and dinners with members of the group we benefit immensely.

I also recognize this type of investment, especially when you're just starting out or in the midst of some sort of reorganization may be too steep. We all know the expression, "Where there's a will there's a way." A creative alternative of the foregoing, for instance, could be you stay relatively local to and engage other establishments to your benefit and theirs.

The simplest way you could benefit from other restaurateurs in your area is to arrange dinner at a restaurant you respect and chat up the owner over a drink at the bar or at table side. Be open. Ask questions. Generally speaking people love to talk, and more often than not people love to talk about themselves and their success. Allow friendly conversation to develop, see where it leads and then you will have the power to direct the questioning.

Obviously you need to have some social grace here and be able to gauge responses, but I encourage you not to be afraid to ask very direct questions like (Please keep in mind your questions might be more targeted, especially if the restaurant purports to cater to a particular need, is a specialist in a style, or has a broad and unique menu…)

- Where do you buy (fish, cheeses, beef, etc.…)? This is especially important if the restaurant purports to be a specialist in a particular food or style of foods.
- Who is your beverage purveyor?
- Are breads/desserts baked on premises and did you start out that way or grow into it? Why?
- Are you happy with your gas, snow removal, and/or waste removal companies?
- What POS system do you use? Have you used others? What did/don't you like about it?
- How do you collect guest data?

Another way in which you could take smaller strides towards a Mastermind group locally is to invite your local restaurateurs to meet to discuss local economy, needs, seasonal issues, etc.… You might develop some sort of promotional tour of the local restaurants like a restaurant week. You could all agree on a theme and a fixed discount for those who participate. Your local restaurants could develop and agree on participating in some sort of worthy fundraiser that would benefit the community. The PR gained for all of the restaurants working together for a common community goal could be priceless advertising for all involved.

Some last words of advice here. Competition is a good thing because without it we're not pushed to be creative, innovative and better than we were yesterday. In all of what I've suggested you need to be confident that no one can do what you do, because you're the one who created the niche. In your confidence you can give away some of the things you've developed but don't give away the proverbial farm either. Your confidence and expertise in your product will come through and by leading the way in your community, with careful planning you could reap great rewards on many levels, not the least of which being a busier restaurant.

Mistake #27:   You don't participate in community service.

I THINK WE ARE all familiar with the expression, *"What goes around comes around."* As a business in the community I get hit up for donations for various causes and events on a nearly constant basis. I also know many business owners who would never consider making a donation let alone several per year. I've often heard, "I keep giving, but who's going to help me?"

I operate on a relatively simple set of rules.

- I have to believe in the cause, charity/organization asking for the donation.
- The individual asking for the donation must come in personally to discuss the need.
- I strategize the donation so it can generate traffic in the restaurant and do this by giving a $10 gift certificate as a base donation to nearly all who come to ask.
- Based upon the first two bullets, if something comes up I feel very passionate about or strikes me as having more importance, then I may give up to a $100 gift certificate. I stay alert to these types of events during the course of the year.

Generally speaking, I've found most if not all organizations looking for donations are very happy to receive a gift certificate because of the means by which they will be distributing the donation.

Honesty here is a good policy as well. We explain it is our hope that in giving a donation there is a mutual benefit because the business will be mentioned as part of the award to the person who receives the gift certificate, and that we will gain additional visitors as well. There is nothing wrong with creating a win-win for all parties involved. It's not truly feasible for me to simply give away vast amounts of money, but I am keen to make a wise investment.

Bear in mind giving is not always about making it work in your favor from a financial perspective and this is a call you have to make. Our first meal served was providing food to those who needed help. We were slated to open our doors New Year's Eve in 2004 and before we opened officially as a commercial establishment my wife and I held a soup kitchen on Christmas Day 2003. We intended to do this every year regardless of the cost because we felt/feel it is vitally important to help our community in this way: especially for those who need the assistance during the holiday season. At the time of this writing we've done thirteen years of soup kitchens, coordinated with a local social service agency.

Our tenth anniversary soup kitchen was the first one in which the community donated enough to cover the entire cost of this yearly project. Frankly, we were amazed, and humbled by this seriously generous level of community involvement. Regardless of getting the support or not, we will keep on providing the 500 plus dinners we make, package, and deliver, because this is one of things that is just, THAT important to us.

As with much of what I've written in this book, it's all up to you. You're the one with the keys to your own success. How you choose to comport yourself is up to you.

Mistake #28: You don't require a jacket and tie, so why is your food wrapped in that attire?

WE CAN ALL RELATE to trends and fads: bell bottom pants, Rubik's cube, disco, the Walkman, triple stuffed Oreos, Olestra®, Atkins Diet, etc.… Things done thirty years ago can readily make a comeback. These trends occur in every industry and the restaurant world is no different. If you've been going to trade shows or reading trade journals for any length of time, this notion should be apparent. Each season there is some new "hot" food, a new technology, décor motif, and seating style…

There are multiple things at stake here. Your menu items in particular may not represent current food/eating trends and be so far outdated and/or staid that you're keeping new guests from discovering your "genius" and not growing your business. You've already been warned you can't simply go with every trend there is, especially if it is outside the vocabulary, personality, style of your restaurant. Perhaps the most important reason for this simple fact is; it is far too costly and time consuming to move from one thing to the next. Even the biggest names in the restaurant world don't simply trundle off with the next "big food thing". They may however invest some time to see how they may incorporate a new trend into their style without having to completely reinvent their entire world to do it.

I reiterate here, in order to keep apprised of new trends you need to be immersed in the trade show/trade journal activities previously mentioned. You need to be very clear about whom you are, what your mission and vision are, while also being thoughtful and creative. Not too tall an order to accomplish and very doable.

You're not limited to "food" here by the way. Among the excellent things trending in the past few years have been the craft beer and spirit industry. There are more craft brewers and distillers than ever before. Local in this case could be a neighboring county for you, but also taking pride in those things produced in the good 'ole US of A makes for excellent sales and marketing. It does not have to take a lifetime of learning to make additions and/or transitions in your restaurant from the major known brands to smaller production spirits (vodka, whiskey, gin...) or beers that are of higher quality and equal or better flavor profiles.

The farm-to-table buzz and the locally sourced product push are excellent current trends to capitalize on. Perhaps, you have a local farm known for and/or eager to get its superior quality products into the market place. You could revamp one of your dishes to either feature the product in question regularly or offer it seasonally as a special item as the circumstances dictate. As already mentioned, and worth repeating, you'll be revamping or introducing something relevant and new to your current offerings, while at the same time open a new avenue for cross-promotion and "community minded" awareness.

I've just pointed out a couple ways of doing this. My successes in this process have created something of an added thrill about our offerings: both food and beverage based. As a result of going down this road I am able to offer some "harder" to obtain items our guests now come in to partake of because they are unable to find the item(s) on their own (my staff is instructed to happily share purveyor information with our guests.)

At the outset, I approach all of this from the win-win perspective. I have been developing and refining these types of moves in trend for years. You can make this commitment as quickly or as slowly as you see fit. Bear in mind the high side potential, self-marketing and cross-promotional benefits you have in your power during the process. The idea here is hopefully obvious: learn, seek, think, create, and act.

Mistake #29:   You don't have the skill to market for new staff.

YOU NEED HELP. Almost all profitable businesses require excellent support staff. Generally speaking, unless you're operating a lunch truck and are a one man band so-to-speak, you need help to run any successful business. You couldn't possibly manage tables, get drinks, take orders, and then cook the food all by yourself. The tried and true method of placing want ads still holds today. Where you place your job ads and how you write them is very important. Craigslist, the local paper, and word of mouth are more than likely your best bets for getting new staff in the door. If you're already an established restaurant and have a couple of solid and consistently high performing staff members, asking them to refer candidates can be potentially a good thing.

However, going this route still requires/demands that you conduct the hiring and evaluation process as you would for any other potential hire. It's your business and you owe anyone a thing. You must remain in the seat of power for this to be successful.

When you write job adverts for new employees the tone and manner of the wording needs to be in accord with your mission and vision. Many business owners don't necessarily give true consideration to the ads they place for new staff. In reality, this is yet another form of advertising your business. You need to do this thoughtfully and creatively as it is one more way in which to get your name, reputation, and personality as a business out there.

Unlike other businesses I've been able to minimize our share of "revolving door" syndrome when it comes to hiring and retaining staff. Generally speaking my staff have been with us long term and many of those who've moved onto other things are willingly available if the need arises. My job ads are deliberately evocative. Here are a couple of examples.

Sample Ad #1

Superstars Wanted

Aroma Thyme Bistro in Ellenville is looking for another superstar to join our wait staff team. If you're not a superstar, please don't apply. It takes dedication to be part of our team. If you feel you have superstar qualities we want to hear from you. Aroma Thyme Bistro is a Green Certified© restaurant that has one of the best-stocked bars in the Hudson Valley. We pride ourselves in local, organic and healthier gourmet food. If you would like to be part of our family, please email us.

Sample Ad #2

Line Cook Needed

Busy restaurant in Ellenville constantly overwhelmed with unqualified and unreliable applicants. Restaurant needs a well-organized and detail oriented line cook.

Do you get the gist of what you're reading here? You want to cull the deadweight from the herd right off the bat. You're prompting a self-selection process. By using evocative key words, "well-organized", "detail oriented", "team player", "superstar", "loyal", you're throwing down the gauntlet, so to speak. You're evoking a sense of pride, self-motivation, ownership, perhaps an air of exclusivity, and the potential for belonging to something important in your candidates right off the bat. This is a powerful lure.

Be prepared because the hiring/search process will almost never work out perfectly, but it does work. Also, you need to be aware that the hiring process is expensive. It's time, energy, effort up front, aside from the actual dollars spent in advertising for new staff. Add to this, new staff training, the time it takes to get the newbie up-to-speed and independent, the potential for loss of revenue, poor reviews, and host of other knotty details. You can see why hiring is so very important to get "right" the first time as much as humanly possible.

You need to be able to deliver on what you publicize about your restaurant and you must be honest about your limitations as a business and a boss. If you're not an easy person to get along with, then you better make up for it in other ways so you're able to retain staff and breed loyalty. If you don't, then you'll find yourself a slave to your business and have created nothing more than a lifetime job for yourself instead of being able to grow a business and be an entrepreneur.

Mistake #30:   Interviewing: You don't know how to hold an audition.

INTERVIEWING IS A SKILL business owners don't necessarily have the first clue about. While you are in the position of hiring someone who needs a job, many more individuals understand the interview process is as much about the potential hire interviewing the potential employer for a good match.

By now you know the saying, "You can only make a first impression once." As the entrepreneur, if you're interview skills are poor, your demeanor mousy and lacking confidence, then don't expect to hire well unless you live under some giant cloud of dumb luck.

If you want well spoken, presentable, energetic self-motivated people working for you, then you best be able to present yourself in that manner during the interview process. Because interviewing is a process, you need to have a well-developed set of procedures you can follow consistently. Certainly you're not going to get this perfect each and every time, but you do want to be prepared to the point where you significantly minimize your mistakes and maximize the moment to bring out the best of who you are as a boss and bring out the best of what your potential candidate has to offer.

As stated over and over, you must embody your mission and vision during the interview process. Articulating this clearly will in and of itself set a particular tone and help guide the interview. Some things to keep in mind when interviewing new staff for your business might include:

- Before bringing someone in for a face-to-face interview always pre-qualify the individual over the phone so you don't waste your time later. If the job seeker passes this step, then bring them in for an interview.

- Establish a set list of questions for each position (hostess, wait staff, kitchen…). There are resources around for this so you don't need to reinvent the wheel. Consistency in asking the same essential questions of each candidate provides you the greatest insight when selecting from multiple candidates. It makes for a fair and level playing field. Certainly, you're free to ask follow-up questions and should do so, in addition to asking for specific clarifications when needed. Consider keeping the list to about ten essential/critical questions, but have at least fifteen to select from.

- Many businesses live by the notion of hiring slow and firing fast. Even if your gut tells you the candidate is perfect, you MUST let every potential new staff member know there is an "audition" or "trial" period. You want total control when selecting who represents your business and you want to be able to have an easier out early on if needing to let someone go.

- Engage your senior staff when you're looking to hire new staff in the same or similar positions. Do this for either part of, or the whole interview process. This goes back to trusting your staff and empowering them in developing a greater sense of "ownership" in your business. By developing this aspect of your leadership style and cultivating this level of trust in your staff you will breed deeper loyalty and stability in the long term. Just remember to convey that their input is advisory only and you retain the right of veto and being able to have the final say. Balance in accomplishing this successfully is important and comes with practice.

- Set very high expectations during the interview process so you can weed out weaker individuals at the outset. Having a candidate self-select out of the process is an excellent way of knowing who you may or may not be dealing with.

- ALWAYS ask for and check references. You are limited as to what can and can't be asked when checking references of a job candidate. Check labor laws regarding this so you don't get yourself or the person you're calling into trouble.

- Always provide the candidate with a job description. It ought to be obvious, but this makes the statement that you're organized and you know what you're doing. Additionally, it lets the candidate know what they can expect. Many job descriptions I've seen over the years have included a last statement that reads as follows, "Other duties/tasks as necessary." There are very little, if any tasks in the restaurant our wait staff has not done at some point. You want to ensure you have the flexibility to get the job done, especially in a time of need. You never want to hear, "That's not my job."

Remember, you're providing the jobs. You're the one in a significant position of leadership. Be candid, honest, clear, organized, and upfront during the interview process. If you're the least bit unsure of how to interview, then have a trusted partner or associate sit with you the first few times you do this. Practice interviewing skills with a friend or two and have them rate your abilities. If you end up having someone else sit with you during the interview process, explain to your candidates who the additional person is so that everyone is clear. If you have senior staff sit with you during an interview, develop a debriefing sheet for each candidate so you can rate and discuss each of the potential candidates before making a final decision.

Ultimately when you hire someone for your business you've entered into a relationship with them. You must listen very carefully to how questions are answered and how they're not answered. Press for clarification to your questions and even challenge candidates with their answers when appropriate. If you have good people skills and think you're a good judge of character with a proven track record, and you don't get a good feeling with a candidate, then you need to go with your gut. You don't want to enter into a "relationship" with someone you feel at the outset will not be a good match.

As I've already stated, in the end a bad hire will cost you time, energy, and money. I've outlined having an exit strategy and can't stress enough to never make promises during an interview. Always leave yourself in control with some sort of out.

If you take the time and energy to develop your interviewing and hiring practices before setting about the task of actually interviewing and hiring, you will find yourself with more stable, productive, and long term staff. Ultimately this will allow you to put your energies into maximizing your bottom line.

Mistake #31:   Performance Reviews. You don't know how to be honest with your staff.

YOU'RE PROBABLY FAMILIAR WITH the adage, "Familiarity breeds contempt." You're the boss. You may be a great guy or gal and you may have developed tight relationships with your staff. This however can be the two-edged sword implied in the above adage. So I'll restate the second statement of this paragraph, "You're the boss". Developed friendships and tight relationships aside, this is your business, you have expectations, and you can't let your feelings get in the way of demanding high quality service or performance from your staff. This is your livelihood. You need to set in place a system of formal and regular reviews of your staff's performance.

As with a structured interview process, this is not some willy-nilly thing. Performance reviews should be informed by the job descriptions you've provided to your staff. As with any labor oriented task, there are resources available to you (some really good ones for free), that will keep you from having to reinvent the wheel and thereby saving you time.

Have a set of scripted questions for these meetings, keep track of your meetings, and conduct them at least four times per year. Remember I emphasized having a way out if you misjudged a potential hire during the audition/trial period? Well this is your way out if someone you hired has become an issue after the initial audition period.

During your one-on-one meetings you will ask questions that promote self-reflection and self-review in your staff. You want to gauge how each staff member answers these based upon your observations, expectations, and guest feedback as would be the case with the reviews your restaurant may receive from your comment cards, emails, and/or various review sites.

If you're not having regular staff meetings then you'll need to do this as well. During my staff meetings, which are mandatory and held weekly, my wife and I ask self-reflective questions of our staff, share both positive and negative feedback (guest motivated and management observed), and use all of this as the proverbial teachable moment.

Questions asked during staff meetings and one-to-one review meetings may include:

- What was a standout moment during the last couple of weeks/month personally and while you were working?

- What was a moment you'd like to do over or improve upon during the last couple of weeks/month personally and while you were working?

- Describe a happy customer moment.

- What was an, "Oh, SNAP moment?" (This is our in-house code for "Service Never AS Perfect" and can be wait staff, owners, or kitchen staff. It's our way of recognizing and promoting work done above and beyond.)

- What is a strength you have and how can you improve upon it?

- What is a weakness you have and how can you improve upon it?

- What can we do to help you achieve better results here at work?

- Are there skills you have we have not yet recognized you for?

If it is not obvious, we're not about coming down hard on our staff, but raising them up. Yes, there are consequences for mistakes and poor behavioral choices, as there should be in any business. My wife and I earnestly try to walk out improvement and learning experiences versus taking punitive actions for mistakes. Our guests frequently comment how at home and welcome they feel when they come to dine with us. This can only occur when there is solid leadership growing individuals who believe in our mission and vision. We have discovered that the review process helps to keep us on our toes, keep our mission and vision fresh before us, and it helps to build a level of consistency, expectation, and quality we only dreamed of when we started in this business so many years ago. I'm happy to report and encourage you to discover this does not have to be a dream, but a functional, positive, and profitable reality.

Mistake #32: You don't take advantage of instant replay: check those references.

WHEN YOU'VE GONE TO the trouble of hiring someone, checking their references, unless you know them personally needs to be considered a non-negotiable. Frankly, even if you "know" them personally, it's still an excellent idea to check his/her references. While you may know one side of the person, you've not had any experience with them as an employee and this can be an entirely different matter altogether.

Reiterating a sentiment previously stated: This is your business, your investment, your reputation, your potential joy and your potential headache. If you get this far in the interview process and are duped by someone who can interview really well, not check their references, and find out later they are a lousy employee; you're going to find yourself starting at square one again.

Because of the Internet, Facebook, and other social media websites, it's relatively easy to research who is sitting in front of you, aside from calling their listed references. It is astounding how "publicly" people live their lives today and anything you find out about an applicant in any "public" forum is fair game for questioning, concern, and/or clarification. The individual has essentially given up some of their right to privacy once something has become part of the World Wide Web. If your applicant's email address is smokesalotofpot@houseofbongs.com then you know you may have a potentially serious issue and bringing this up in an interview is fair game.

Another cause for concern would the applicant's inability to provide you with at least three professional references, as opposed to three personal references. Bear in mind hiring a new bus person, who is a high school student, might be an exception to this rule, though he/she could still provide you with teacher references to speak to the individual's character.

I am not a labor law expert by a long shot and you will need to know how to proceed within your state's guidelines. The bottom line is, you must absolutely follow up and make calls to the references provided by your applicants. The time you spend doing this, as with anything else where good preparation is required, will only save you headaches and time and effort in the end.

Mistake #33: You don't invest in your largest expense by training your staff.

ART OF THE AROMA THYME BISTRO mission is educating our guests about who we are, when they come to dine with us. This education is either reinforced with our regular guests or imparted to newbies to the restaurant. Frankly, our menu can be a bit overwhelming and our catalog of beverage offerings is massive. During an average shift, our staff will encounter at least one new guest who asks for something we don't serve. I will not stand for the flat, conversation ending response of, "We don't have it."

It leaves nothing for the guest to hold onto and generally creates a level of disappointment that could cause this new potential lifetime guest to not come back. I'm in business to have repeat business, not one offs. When we tell a guest we don't do something or don't offer something, we immediately follow up with something that leads to further conversation and education. Without careful and thorough training, the average wait staff will be unable to initiate the follow-up.

A simple example: I don't offer any "light" beers. I offer beers that are lighter in texture and flavor, but not in the traditional marketing sense of a "light" beer. My wait staff is well versed in our beverage catalog, so they can make very quick conversation with a new guest to ascertain what it is he/she enjoys drinking, flavor preferences, etc.... Because I generally have nine beers on tap, my wait staff will start by tasting the guest on a couple of these offerings. Nearly one hundred percent of the time, they quickly narrow down the choices so the guest gains a new experience they wouldn't have had otherwise; they've gotten a bit of an education; and they've been introduced to a new dining experience. During the whole process, my staff never judges and they make the experience as pleasant and fun as possible.

Go into just about any restaurant or sit at any bar and you'll find most wait staff and bartenders have no serious clue as to what they're serving, where it's from, what it tastes like or even care for that matter. In a business that is supposed to be about service, I've experienced far too many places that make it feel like the staff is doing you a favor about tasting something I'm going to drop good money on. Needless to say, I find this a huge turnoff and a serious red flag about the establishment in which I've chosen to dine or drink.

Recall my instruction on "giving to get." Offering the guest the experience to taste a beverage and have a potentially new experience outside of their "norm", ultimately costs you nothing, nada, zilch. If you've priced your menu correctly you will gain profit in the immediate and potentially gain yet another lifetime guest.

Get the point here. Train, train, train your staff. You want them to excel. You want your service to go above and beyond that of any other establishment in your community. You want your guests to rave about your place and recommend it to everyone they know. So I repeat. If your staff isn't properly trained then you're going to lose and lose big time.

The good news is you probably have senior staff members who are well trained (hopefully), and they should be enlisted in this process. You want to replicate their successes and strengths in the strengths of each of your other staff. By using these members of your team, you will be deepening their engagement/ownership of your business, further empowering them, and demonstrating and acknowledging their worth to your organization by entrusting them with contributing to the training of new staff.

Other ways in which you can train your staff is to hold workshops on various aspects of your business so as to broaden their experiences overall. It shouldn't be all that difficult to have your vendors (both food and beverage) sponsor these types of things periodically throughout the year.

Utilize part or all of your staff meeting time to role playing so that good behaviors/scenarios can be demonstrated and critiqued. Conversely, you can conduct role playing situations which demonstrate negative behaviors/scenarios. Allow time for critique and discussion. Along these lines, use your online reviews and comment card feedback as a training tool. You can create a weekly quiz regarding knowledge and source of food items on your menu.

Over the last couple of years, I've created a number of training videos on nearly all aspects of service and comportment in my business. This has become a mandatory part of the introductory phase of training for all new staff members. These videos are posted to our website and it allows the new staff member to watch and absorb the information at their own pace.

Hopefully you have clear expectations for the kind of service you want to get from your employees. If you don't prepare a training plan for your staff you're going to end with very inconsistent and poor service overall in your restaurant. This applies to both the front of house and your kitchen. Regardless of where your strength(s) lay, there are resources to help you.

Mistake #34:   You don't take time out to play with
your staff.

O WNING A RESTAURANT, even if you're
passionate about it is no walk in the park most
days. Regardless of the size of your establishment
we advocate making use of training games that can
contribute to building a team atmosphere and pay great
dividends when things get tough. As an addendum to the
section on training we mention here that games are fun and are
an excellent tool to team and knowledge building. You can add
to your staff meetings or pre-shift meetings a game like menu
bingo. These games can be played at meetings and during the
regular work shift.

Games like menu bingo, name the spice, or name the spirit can
make for some good clean fun and provide some training in the
process. By conducting a periodic game, you're also building a
culture of professional ease. You're creating a message to your
staff that your restaurant is worth giving all they have to it. You
can use games to team build and provide some friendly
competition among your staff to motivate sales.

As previously mentioned I'm highly involved with Royalty
Rewards©. Our staff knows how important this is to our success
and to theirs. I had not intended for this to happen, but after a
staff meeting that reiterated the importance of gaining new
qualified signups for the program, our two most senior wait
staff ended up in a very friendly back and forth over the

subsequent couple of months gaining new signups. It was a great boost for their professional relationship, causing them to bond more closely as a team and ultimately the restaurant and our new regulars benefited too.

The book, *Games Trainers Play*, by Edward Scannell & John Newstrom is a great beginning resource for implementing games to create a positive environment. You'll find icebreakers, team building, trust building, and insight building games. Investing in this sort of training activity will be a worthwhile use of your time that will return positive benefits to you, your business, and your staff.

III.   Advertising/Promotion

Mistake #35:   You don't have a billboard.

SOME RESTAURANTS DO THIS very well and some don't do it at all. The cost to do this kind of marketing is virtually free. It's called, *"Four Walls Marketing."* This is where you take advantage of bathroom, door space, window, wall, and table space to advertise your upcoming events, promotions, and specials.

If you're doing themed events then this is especially beneficial. If you remember in one of the earlier tips I spoke of conducting themed dinners, events, weekly specials, and other cool events to get people through your door. Sadly, lots of restaurants never take advantage of the marketing power within the confines of their own restaurant. It's as simple as printing out a flyer and posting it on the door of your bathroom(s) or making table tents or putting a large chalkboard/sandwich board on the sidewalk outside of your restaurant. Partnering with your vendors can often result in getting some of these notices printed professionally and for free.

Let's say you're going to promote a lobster special/night and pair it with a particular wine and/or beer, then you may go to the wine/beer vendor and ask them for the artwork to support the event. They may even be willing to provide you with a promotional poster. In the end they are making an investment in advertising their own product(s). They want to make money as well by having sales. Doesn't this sound familiar?!

Another great strategy is putting smaller promotional cards in your check presenters. Every one of your guests eventually has to pay their bill. We put various size cards, serving different purposes in our check presenters. Items I include are the latest promotion, usually a square colored card, our business card, a feedback/comment card, and a request for a "free party". Everything in the presenter is professionally done, sized to catch the guest's attention, and at the very least create a sense of curiosity.

Marketing doesn't begin and end with newspaper ads, mailers and radio spots. You have space in your restaurant and a captive audience on a regular basis. Don't waste that space, use it creatively communicate what you're doing to your advantage. As with everything else make certain your staff are well informed and articulate about what is going on so they can also be a "billboard" informing your guests and contributing more thoroughly to your success.

Mistake #36:   You don't know how or when to tell a good story.

A MAJOR OPPORTUNITY TOO often missed is not telling a story to your guests. We're not talking about *Hansel and Gretel* here. Every good business has any number of stories that can be told to its clientele/guests. These stories provide education, insight, humor, and potentially make for incredible sales gains. Whether it's the wine you've selected for your list, the bourbons you serve, or the food choices you've made for your menu, there is a story, a history, and perhaps a bit of intrigue to be shared.

One story could be how you came to open your business and how you came to have a love of food and cooking. Was this a part of your family history or did something happen along the way causing your eyes to be opened to the amazing world of gastronomy? The story could be about your philosophical take on how food is prepared and how this has informed your mission as a restaurateur. The current trend of local/farm to table fare could be ripe (yes, pun intended) with lots of stories to share and in the process you'd be cross-promoting a part of your community that may be unknown to many of your guests. People want to know where their food is from and what's in it.

When you engage your guests in the story, whatever it may be with regard to your menu items, you are creating, perhaps unknowingly, a deep emotional connection to the food or drink in which your guests are partaking. People make many of their purchasing decisions based on emotions.

By not telling the stories you're missing out. We suggest you start small. You must be able to deliver truth in these stories and do it well. Start with one or two beverage items and one or two menu items unique to your establishment. Make sure you know the details well, tell the truth, and at the same time create a bit of mystique.

We have an extensive menu at Aroma Thyme Bistro and an even more extensive beverage catalog. One of the stories shared with our guests is about one of our desserts. When my wife and I got engaged we had Bananas Foster: one of our favorite desserts. I revised the traditional recipe so it would be equally as delicious as the traditional version but equally important fit the style, mission/vision of our restaurant. Our servers share this story and the manner in which we make it (ingredients and all) with our guests. The story provides a purpose and an intimacy for it being on our menu. You might have a local seasonal item you obtained by foraging your local forest or by finding it at the local farmer's market. Your servers need to know the details so this can be shared with your guests.

Another benefit of telling the story can be the resulting up sell. Our wine catalog has an asterisk next to each vineyard my wife and I have visited. One Saturday lunch a guest inquired about a bottle of wine from a particular region of Italy. It happened that this particular wine was from a vineyard I visited with my wife on one of our trips. I shared the story of our trip and the process in which the vintner made the wine and the result was an up sell from a $30 bottle of wine to one priced at $120 per bottle. It wasn't my intention to necessarily up sell the guest, it simply happened as a result of telling the story.

I can't stress enough you never lie telling a story to your guest. A lie told is exceptionally difficult to recover from. Your guests come to your restaurant in part because they trust they are going to have a good time and get great value. Additionally people do not want to be forced into buying something or sold something. Your guests will respond to a story though and very often this can lead to additional sales and the purposeful cultivation of your unique place in your business community.

Be proud of the reason you came to be chef and/or business owner. You had/have a dream. You have a story. You have a uniqueness you bring to the market place and this singularity needs to be shared. Capitalize on your story. Share it with your guests. Make certain your staff knows it, so they can share it when asked. It is the underlying song for your success and something people can easily relate to.

Mistake #37:   Your guests don't really know who you are.

A SLIGHTLY DIFFERENT ANGLE on the story telling aspect of your business is allowing the guests into your world. This tip focuses on who you are and who your family is and how to communicate that to your guests. Demystifying the notion you're some super human (well no one is really) and approachable is important. Oft times being perceived as successful is synonymous with being unapproachable. It is my opinion you need to let your guests know you're as real a person as they are. Of course, you need to remain real professional and real respectful.

Your family can be an excellent source of guest relations and a significant part of the fabric of your success. I'm not suggesting you overuse them in your marketing. Recall I've said your guests want to be part of the "in crowd" and part of the success of your restaurant. Careful use of your family and judicious sharing of information about them can be a very powerful tool to promoting your restaurant and furthering your success. For example, our children have grown up in the restaurant and many of our guests, especially our "lifetime" guests have seen our children grow. We have allowed some into more private areas of our lives because these guests have also have become closer "friends".

A less personal example and one easy to highlight is the fact that our daughter has been riding horses since she was six. Now seventeen years old (at the time of this writing), she's attained success at a competitive level. As we've discovered, by simply sharing this information with a variety of guests as a natural part of conversation with them, we've learned some are involved with horses or have been in the past. As a result, though we certainly didn't share information with the intent of receiving something in mind, one of our guests very generously gave her an expensive saddle no longer being used in their family. This would never have happened if we were not open to the notion of sharing who we are, what we do, and what our family is involved in.

I'm an avid runner and my son is an amazing athlete. We've run several races together in our community. As a result of sharing with our guests, I've learned there are quite a few avid runners among our regulars. Sharing this part of our lives provides purposeful, easy conversation with our guests and provides them an opportunity to be part of our lives beyond the restaurant.

One year, when our children were younger, we had them hand write letters to our guests as part of a promotional campaign. This led to a fantastically successful and positive response. These examples provide significant win-win situations for the success of our business.

The bottom line is you are part of the community. In point of fact owning and operating a successful business, particularly a restaurant, makes you a meeting place for the community at large. Your commitment to your community and sharing who you are keeps you from being a stranger in your own home.

Mistake #38:   You blew your entire advertising
budget in one place.

I'VE HEARD MANY A restaurateur and business
owner say they didn't have a budget for marketing or
they've set aside $1000/month for print ads. It should be
clear at this point this mentality makes no sense
whatsoever. All of your advertising efforts need to be filtered
through the lens of return on investment (ROI) and not some
standard and expected means of advertising.

To be clear, ROI is simply how much of your investment you
will make back over "x" period of time. The shorter the time
taken for you to make back your initial investment the better
your ROI and the better the idea was. If it takes longer for you
to make the investment back plus a profit, then you will need to
refine/rethink the rationale for the investment; review the
timing of the launch for the particular promotion; or perhaps
scrap it all together.

More concretely, if the thousand dollars you're investing every
month for marketing is returning $20,000 in sales/annum then
you may consider expanding your market reach or increasing
your monthly outlay for the type of advertising you're doing.
Your job is to determine your best marketing strategy. Needless
to say, your marketing goal is to get the biggest returns possible
on your investment. We never conduct a marketing campaign
or promotion without tracking and measuring its outcome: just

like we never put a dish on menu without calculating the cost first and the subsequently monitoring of its sales/profits.

In fact, we can track marketing expenditures and profits by month longitudinally from year to year for any given month. The power in this long term data/knowledge is nearly without value. Simply hanging up your shingle and waiting for guests to meander their way through your door is very likely going to make you a statistic, and not the good kind. Remember you're running a business and you're in it to make money and support yourself and/or your family.

Marketing is not about shameless self-promotion, though having healthy pride in your establishment and your accomplishments is indeed very important. Marketing must be thoughtful, targeted, and upheld by the use of various forms of data which you must obtain. Your marketing needs to be considered more in terms of a "guaranteed gamble". Your investment of time, energy, and money takes on new meaning if you consider it in the following manner. If you spend $1 on creating a postcard you send out promoting a new event based upon feedback from guest comment cards; you have a very good chance of making $40-$70 on that $1 investment. While nothing in life is guaranteed, doing nothing and relying solely on good food is a rather significant risk in and of itself.

IV.   Cooking

Mistake #39:   Your regular menu gets boring.

IT IS IMPOSSIBLE TO please everyone all of the time and trying to do so is an enormous waste of time. You have a personality. Your restaurant has a personality. You need to play to your strengths. You also want to endeavor to create a little bit of something for everyone (at least most everyone), this way you'll make it more attractive for a wider array of people to come and dine at your establishment, even if it is outside of their "perceived" comfort zone.

On the one hand, your guests love your steak and on the other some ask for more variety. How you balance specials against long term popular regular items are important to keep your steady guests happy, while at the same time attracting new ones. Make your restaurant fun and exciting. Do different things. Give your guests reasons to come back over and over again. Too many restaurants just offer their regular menu every night. It might be enough to keep your restaurant packed at first, but overtime you'll find "menu fatigue" setting in because you will have developed a particular reputation that only happens over time. Creatively changing it up a bit will keep your guests intrigued, keep your chef engaged, and keep the staff engaged and on their toes.

I learned a long time ago as a young Executive Chef that guests will come in more often for different events and themes. My very first theme dinner was *Titanic Night*. This was when the movie *Titanic* was playing in the theaters still. The manager gave me the idea and I ran with it. We charged a lot of money for our guests to participate. It was fun researching the menu items offered on the Titanic. Do some research and you'll find a book regarding the last meal served on the Titanic. Our guests dressed up for the occasion. It turned out to be a spectacular night. As the new chef I was an instant hit with the guests and this motivated me to keep coming up other themed events.

As a result, we implemented weekly specials and monthly special events. Examples of these include an "all you can eat crab legs" night and monthly beer or wine dinners. At our current restaurant, Aroma Thyme Bistro, we do all sorts of themed events regularly. Remember these events must fit the mission and vision of your restaurant otherwise you're venturing too far from your strengths and will be at risk for not being able to effectively and confidently deliver the goods.

Some of our most popular annual events have been and continue to be: Belgium Independence Day (July), Twin Lobster Bake (August), Beer and Cheer Beer Share (December), 99 Bottles of Beer on the Bar Grand Beer Tasting (October), 99 Bottles of Wine on the Bar Grand Wine Tasting (January), Mardi Gras week, Drinko de Mayo (yes a whole month's long celebration), Romance Week (taking advantage of Valentine's Day for a whole week: you may even save a relationship or two with the "extended" permission to celebrate on a different day) and Nurses' Week.

We conduct regular monthly themed events including a beer dinner/tasting and a wine dinner/tasting. In addition to the aforementioned "all you can eat" crab legs night, every Monday night is lobster night and every Tuesday guests can enjoy half priced Margaritas. You get the point: creativity and variety all within our base of strength.

Mistake #40:   You're the best chef in town, but this doesn't qualify you to run a successful business. Cooking should be the last part of your job.

I HAVE SEEN SOME of the best chefs fail at opening their own restaurant. Being a great chef, a master baker or having a reputation as being the best maître d' at the local country club in town are not qualifications to open up a business. Those are just a small element of running a successful business. By no means am I downplaying the skills of a master baker, chef extraordinaire, or a maître d' who is able to make absolutely everyone feel at home. Owning and operating a successful business requires totally different skills and determination. Good food and service is not enough to keep people coming in the door anymore. You have to be a marketing maniac.

There have been a nearly innumerable number of good chefs who've gone into business and quickly gone out of business because they did not know how to run a business. While good food and good service is the core of your efforts, there is a litany of details requiring your concerted and focused attention. Among these details include and are not limited to the following:

- Ordering food, liquor, and supplies
- Taking and maintaining inventory
- Purchasing equipment

- Purchasing insurance
- Negotiating contracts with vendors
- Advertising, hiring and training staff
- Managing and motivating staff

These examples simply touch the surface. There's a whole other list of things that deal only with guest relations. If you simply want to be a chef, then consider working for someone else. If you want to be a business owner/restaurateur, who creates jobs for others and a high level of success for yourself and your family, then you need to learn how to be a good marketer, spokesperson, and savvy customer relations expert.

Most restaurant owners don't realize what business they are actually in. Of course you own a restaurant so one would assume you are in the restaurant business. This truth is only part of the story. The remaining part is you are in the marketing business. Your first job should be to market and promote your restaurant. Now some of you have the good fortune of having a fabulous location. But some of these locations can cost significant amounts of money.

Consider owning and operating a restaurant in a major city like Manhattan, New York. Most don't have the desire to run a place in that kind of environment. Even if you do have a place with a phenomenal location with naturally high traffic you still have to get people to walk through your doors. You still have to get noticed and you still have to develop a good reputation, which means you have to market yourself. Most of these places still do at minimum an email blast, a Facebook page, a Twitter account or something to be able to communicate and promote what they are doing. The bottom line is that it's all considered marketing and promotion.

Everywhere you go and with everything you do you need to promote your restaurant. Join the local Chamber of Commerce, business group, and/or local economic development committee. My wife and I attend a variety of mixers and meetings yearly. We hand out business cards, menus, and/or promotional certificates. Over time we have grown more confident and comfortable engaging attendees at these events and endeavor to make positive first impressions in order to bring new guests through the door.

Marketing is critical to not simply getting guests into your establishment but it is critical for motivating guests you have had to return to your restaurant over and over again.

Mistake #41:   You think people get their vitamins
and fiber at home.

OR AN INDUSTRY THAT holds the essential elements to one's overall health, more than a few restaurants are nothing more than a complete and utter joke when it comes to the nutrition and dietary needs of their guests. Chew on that thought for a bit. In fact, many culinary schools don't include dietary concerns in their curriculums, much like the training medical doctors receive: they only get a very cursory overview with regard to nutrition and its role in overall health.

Sadly, we live in a society where people are horribly clueless about what they truly require when it comes to daily nutritional needs. They rely solely upon what the major media outlets (funded by Big Agra advertising dollars) dictate they need. At the very least, I strongly believe you need to be educated as to what dietary concerns/allergies/sensitivities your guests may come to you with and be able to accommodate those concerns. If you do this well, and I mean, do this seriously well; you will position your restaurant in a very unique category serving both your guests' needs and your bottom line in very positive ways. Ah, yet another potential win-win scenario. I must offer my caveat again: You must+ do this well. Otherwise you potentially open yourself up to causing significant harm to your guests and you if you screw this up.

Note: This section is by no means meant to be comprehensive in scope but more a tour of some highlights. More detailed research, planning, sourcing of products and designing menu items will be required on your part to successfully pull this off. I take no responsibility here if you make mistakes and harm your guests.

The public's notion of being "vegetarian" has a great deal of variation. By strict definition a vegetarian is one who only eats a plant based diet that may include cooked and raw veggies and fruits, as well as various nuts, seeds, and grains. That said there are those who call themselves vegetarian and eat seafood, cheese and other milk products, and even chicken. The various types of plant ONLY based diets are specific and it is worth learning and understanding the nuances between them. Keyword search terms can include: raw food vegan, fruitarian, lacto-ovo vegetarian, and pescatarian. By taking the initiative to gain this knowledge you will be proactively positioning yourself as unique among your competitors: assuming you elect to offer things that fit these dietary proclivities on your menu.

A case and point from personal experience follows. I attend a local culinary arts program dinner twice a year. The instructor knows I'm a vegetarian and knew I would be attending the event. I sat through a three course dinner watching everyone else eat, while I twiddled my thumbs because they didn't have the capacity, nor the inclination to create something on the fly for me, for the first two courses. I did get a main dish that had some thought put into it, but not enough, especially in light of the wealth of free information available.

It is no longer enough to simply offer a baked potato and steamed broccoli on your menu and call it the vegetarian plate. You will lose a huge amount of market share and return guests if this is what you're thinking. The number of cookbooks, websites, and successful vegetarian restaurants around the country are way too numerous. A simple search for recipes on the Internet alone will be overwhelming and provide you with more than enough inspiration you'll need for a three lifetimes.

Having only a perfunctory knowledge of vegetarianism in all its forms will ultimately be very short sighted. There are those with dietary sensitivities and allergies that could result in serious harm if not fully understood. In this realm you'll need to bone up on: gluten, nut, corn, and berry allergy/sensitivity. You must know the ingredients and packaging/processing of every item coming into contact with or utilized in your menu items.

I can't stress this enough: one mistake could cost you your business if you unintentionally harm someone due to lack of knowledge, care, or concern. This means that you and all of your staff need to be alerted to how important it is to check and recheck before saying you can prepare something for a guest and have it ultimately end badly because of a mistake. Your reputation, livelihood, and investment are at stake.

Our staff is trained to ask, check, and recheck. Even when a staff member is 100% certain that a guest who is gluten free can eat a particular dish, they check with the kitchen to ensure this fact. I'd rather have them check than not. It is always better to be safe than sorry.

Of course, as with anything else you've learned here, it's up to you. I suggest you take the time to know this subject matter, do the necessary research, and create the necessary processes and procedures in your establishment to offer the widest array of choices as possible with the greatest of attention when your guests arrive. As I've stated, you'll end up positioning yourself as truly unique in your area and as a result, over time, your reputation will invariably grow beyond your most immediate sphere of influence. I think it is very worth the effort.

Mistake #42:   Your bar looks like a big box store
midnight sale.

IF YOU AREN'T LIVING in a cave, then you should have noticed there is beverage revolution going on right now and has been for a few years. In point of fact this creative revolution is happening all over the world. The number and variety of small craft breweries and distilleries is dizzying and that's without having a drink or two or three. Distillers are planting themselves near farmers and vineyards. Every state makes wine. Every state makes some form of spirit. Every state craft brews beer. You could conceivably never offer a major brand of beer, wine, or spirit in your restaurant with all that is out there. Plus, you'll never have to apologize for a lack of first class quality either.

I've always had an inclination to offer unique or somewhat obscure items, though in the beginning years I also offered the major brands as well because I thought it was the thing to do. The problem with this dawned on my wife and me about several years ago. We were enabling people to continue to reach for a "recognizable" brand instead of one of the many outstanding offerings we had on the bar.

In one of those "Aha!" moments we decided to simply stop offering major brands. We started with vodka. Back in 2003 it would have been strenuously difficult, if not nearly impossible to readily offer seven USA produced vodkas. When we had our moment of awakening, the market had become robust enough that we could offer a variety of American only vodkas that are unique, well crafted, and cover every taste profile. Subsequent to our shift, we have converts who come to dine with us and look for their new brand of choice. Our staff has become well trained in being able to provide new guests with an alternative to the recognized name brands. We happily provide guests with an impromptu tastings to see which spirit they would like best. With the most modest amount of energy, time, and education, it is truly a simple task to sway someone away from a Big Brand to something new and of equal or higher quality.

I was recently at a local watering hole that had some 100 bottles of various liquors on their bar: almost all of them were the major brand names. Tucked away in the corner I noticed something different and asked the bartender about it. He couldn't speak about it and remarked that no one ever asked for it. DUH! How could anyone ever ask or even know about it when it was left to "hide" in the corner?

If you haven't gotten the point yet...I'm suggesting, encouraging, demanding, cheering you on to be a leader in your business community by sourcing the smaller production products out there. Display your new finds proudly. When you bring in a new small batch beverage, feature it on your menu, display it proudly on the bar, and highlight it in your email blast/newsletter. Make it a big deal. Train your staff to know how to talk about it with your guests. Make suggestions with regard to menu pairings and/or create a promotional special (appetizer, main or dessert) complimenting the flavors of both. Don't get something new to simply tuck it away in a corner on your bar and expect it to sell. Be the expert your competitors are not likely to ever become. For that matter, simply be the expert in all you represent.

V. Personal Growth

Mistake #43: Hey hothead, do you react or do you respond?

I RESPOND TO REVIEWS whether they are positive or negative, but I particularly pay close attention to and respond to the negative ones.

Referring to the topic of social media let me continue the conversation from a slightly different perspective. Social media has provided a nearly immediate, if not actually immediate response to experiences people have. My staff has frequently reported that a guest posted something positive about the restaurant while he/she was sitting at the table eating his/her meal. Of course these are the guests who are in the middle of a very positive experience and have so informed my staff.

On the other hand I'm all too aware that people are more often willing to complain, and do so loudly and publicly than they are willing to invest the time to offer praise. This is a sad statement at best. Further with the increased use of social media and online platforms every guest who comes through the doors of your restaurant is now a potential critic with a waiting public to read their review. These so-called, self-appointed critics have no problem posting their so-called professional opinions. At some level this is terribly unfortunate and it presents both serious issue and potential benefits for your restaurant.

First off, I use our online reviews, both the good and the bad, as learning experiences for me and my staff. My wife and I read and send out unedited comments to our staff regularly through emails and discuss them at our weekly staff workshops. Doing this serves a couple of purposes. We can improve our business by reinforcing the good and highlighting what needs to be improved.

Second, as a business owner, I take the time to respond to all of the feedback we receive, both the good and the bad. It's easier to respond to somebody who is happy about the experience they had at your restaurant; it's not as easy to respond to someone who is angry, upset, and willing to tell the "world" you ruined their anniversary dinner because the fish was overcooked, the server had a crap attitude, or the music was too loud. You can view this sort of complaint as a major burden or a serious opportunity.

For the record I admit it's not fun to respond to these kinds of complaints and there have been a few over the years that have seriously gotten under my skin. I'm human like anyone else and negative feedback can sting. It is however vital to RESPOND and NOT react. I have learned over the years that a careful and thoughtful response more often than not, wins a disgruntled guest and potentially turns them into a raving fan. When you respond to negative reviews you need to consider that the "world" will see you care and you're engaged. You take your work seriously and have pride in your business.

Here are some simple guidelines I've found work regardless of whether or not the complaint is valid in your opinion or not. I must repeat: <u>Responding</u> is almost always and without exception a positive thing. Do not react.

- Wait at least 24 hours before responding. A waiting period will invariably facilitate a more thoughtful response and it provides cool-off-and-think time.

- Bounce the response off your partner or trusted advisor. Simply, don't go this alone. You need to ensure you're not sending off something that will only inflame the situation more.

- Consider offering some sort of compensation, especially if the situation was not brought to your attention while the guest was in the restaurant. If you decide to send something, you might provide a gift certificate of equivalent value to the dish not prepared to the guest's liking or some percent off their next visit.

- If the comment was made publicly, on one of the many travel review sites, then respond publicly.

- If the comment was made privately then keep the response private.

Over the years I have successfully turned many unsatisfied guests (you can't please everyone all the time) around because I have responded to them as opposed to reacted to their negative comments. I have also gained new regulars as a result of this approach because the once dissatisfied guest returned and brought someone new with them.

As a result of our constructive responses to negative reviews, I've had people voluntarily remove their negative review from the site they posted it to. It is not my habit to ask anyone to take a negative review down. I know it is a part of this business and have chosen to take a higher road by developing, growing, and maturing in the manner in which I respond.

Be clear that I am not telling you how to respond. Each incident requires a personal touch tailored appropriately for that situation. Sadly, I have to warn you, there will be times when you will be completely unable to resolve a situation with a disgruntled guest. Think of it this way: There's no talking to crazy. Don't let these types of situations be a source of discouragement. Happily, these types of interactions are few and generally speaking it is obvious to all who read these types of reviews the source is the problem.

If you're not aware of the review sites I've been referring to you will want to research and register yourself on them so when the need arises you can respond. Also, by registering your business on these sites you'll be notified via email when a review is posted. This will save you time from having to search out the information. Additionally, consider setting yourself up with a Google alert based upon the name of your restaurant. Doing so will help you manage your brand and reputation.

The two most prominent websites for restaurant reviews are:

- www.Yelp.com
- www.TripAdvisor.com

Mistake #44: **You don't tell the truth, the whole truth and nothing but the truth.**

PERHAPS THE TITLE SAYS it all. Honesty at table side is the best policy. Taking responsibility for your actions, for those of your staff, for the food, the situation(s), for whatever may come in or go on in your restaurant will go an immeasurably long way with your guests.

For instance, you've been running a fish special all week and you're down to the last few pieces to cook off. Everything has been going gang busters with this special and you discover the last of it has turned or is too small and is unfit for serving. You've got two orders on your line. While the product in question wouldn't make anyone sick, it just doesn't look good. What do you do? You have several choices here:

- Serve the food and see if you can get away with it.
- Don't serve the food and make up some story regarding why.
- Simply send your server back to the table presenting the guest with the menu, the truth and/or an alternative dish.

As a young cook I faced this challenge at a new job. It was my first night at a rather well known and famous resort. I was assigned to work the grill station. Red Snapper was one of the specials for this particular evening's fare. Since it was my very first night I did not have a chance to breathe much less tear apart everything on my new station. (Remember, properly training your staff is critical.) I discovered the snapper was bad. When I told this to the head chef, he directed me to serve the fish anyway. Frankly, I couldn't do it because it was clearly wrong to do so. I called the restaurant manager over and explained the situation. He thanked me for being honest with him and then went out to explain the situation to the guests and the staff.

It's no understatement when you own and operate a restaurant you literally have people's lives in your hands. Improper handling of food, poor staff hygiene, and improper cleaning can cause your business to fail with no chance of recovery.

When confronted with a situation as described, you don't have to tell the guest the fish was old or rotten. You can simply say the fish is not up to your standards and you cannot serve it this evening. You could also say you're not 100% comfortable with the quality of the fish; we'd appreciate it if you ordered something else. Make certain you bring the menu with you so that there is no lag time and service remains smooth.

Unfortunately, all too often many restaurants will allow poor quality items to be cooked because not doing so is a dent in their bottom lines. These establishments don't truly care about their ethics nor do they truly care about their guests' experience. Remember, poor quality food will leave a bad taste (figuratively and literally) in the mouth of the guest.

We believe the absolute best choice to make in situations like this is NEVER compromising the quality of your food, your guests' safety, and the manner in which you present yourself to your guests. You'll find in the end that being honest with your guests will not only be liberating, it will set a very distinct tone for your staff, and it builds an incredible amount of integrity and caché for your business.

Mistake #45:   You don't know how to say no. Try it sometimes, it feels good.

A S RESTAURANT OWNERS WE get lots of requests to do all sorts of things. There are events of all kinds you could potentially host.

When we first opened my wife and I participated in almost every event we were asked to. We thought by doing this we would get more traffic through the restaurant and we thought it was necessary for us to constantly promote ourselves regardless of where it was. While it's true you do have to consistently promote your business, you need to do so thoughtfully and with clear purpose. I'm fortunate that my wife works alongside me taking care of aspects of our business I'm not as strong in skill wise. We're a great team. We're also fortunate to have staff we trust to take care of our business as well.

You may not currently be in this sort of situation and I hope you will eventually find yourself with staff you can trust to the degree we do. My point is you need to take into consideration many factors before you agree to participating in, or promoting a particular event in your restaurant. For us, though we're open on Sundays and we generally do not special on this day. It is the one night during the week precious to my family. When we do have events planned for Sundays, they end by five o'clock in the afternoon so we can plan family time.

Another example of when saying no is a good thing surrounds the mission/vision and culture of your restaurant. Super Bowl Sunday is a huge money maker for many restaurants and bars across the country. While I enjoy many sports, including watching football, we're not a sports bar. In fact we've had many guests seek us out over the years, specifically to avoid all the hoopla surrounding Super Bowl Sunday. Further, though we have a large screen television hanging in our bar area, we don't allow the volume to be turned up at all while guests are in the dining room.

We choose to say no when it comes to promoting Super Bowl Sunday and other like events because they do not represent our ethos. You have a specific goal in mind for your restaurant. You have a theme, a sensibility, and a genre, a whatever. Knowing you can't be all things to all people all of the time, why even bother trudging down that road? Be yourself, and when it's appropriate feel free to be able to say no.

Mistake #46: You don't wait 24 hours before responding to irrationality.

THERE IS AN AWESOME rule of thumb out there regarding wait time. In the education world it has been demonstrated that teachers generally don't wait long enough for their students to respond in class. While a student may wish to answer a question and volunteer to do so, he/she may need time to process before responding. It was discovered teachers waited a measly 1.5 seconds before offering the answer themselves. Yes, you read that correctly, most teachers only wait just a hair more than $1/60^{th}$ of a minute. Research has further demonstrated that waiting 3 whole seconds improved student responses. You may or may not be familiar with the expression, getting something done in a *"New York Minute"*. The implication of course is that it gets done very quickly.

In general most people are not good at waiting and given the generally poor quality of interpersonal relationships most people experience daily, I think you have a good idea of what I'm referring to. So what is the difference between reacting and responding? And, why wait 24 hours before responding?

The notion the customer is always right is quaint, but clearly not true. You will never be able to please everyone all the time and trying to do so will only end in failure. You were just given permission to say no in the previous mistake. You need to play to your strengths and your passion in this business and when that is transgressed by some guest's irrationality: a response is warranted. Note, I did not say your reaction is warranted.

So what's the difference? Simple: choice and intention. When you're at liberty to choose the manner in which you respond to a situation, you are afforded the ability to control the outcome. You are put in the driver's seat; and who doesn't want to be in the driver's seat.

When you're faced with a hostile guest's email or phone call from one who doesn't want to hear reason and you've done everything you know to do to make the situation right; you'll invariably be pissed off beyond belief. Certainly in these situations coming out swinging for the centerfield fence may feel good, but in the end it won't be productive and very likely can have damaging repercussions to your business.

The rule for responding to a bad situation or negative review is 24 hours. During this time, write your rebuttal, counsel with your partner, wife, good friend, and/or trusted staff, beat your pillow, or go hit homeruns at the batting cage: but take the time to burn up your frustration. Once you've done this make certain you take time to carefully reflect on the situation and weigh out a proper and mature response. Remember, once you put something in writing (and we recommend if you respond in writing you get it right the first time) you can't take it back.

If you've done right by the majority of your guests then you'll have the support you require and one negative review, that is clearly an oddity among the really good ones, will shrink into the background as quickly as it came. Time is on your side and by waiting 24 hours to respond, time will be your best friend and ally.

Mistake #47:   You don't have the support you need.

MALL BUSINESSES ARE NOT set up to employ the "on-demand" staff that a corporate giant can. On-demand positions might include: full-time accountants, lawyers, payroll and human resources staff, as well as PR and social media staff. As a small business owner you are chief cook and bottle washer. As an owner/operator I know there were days, especially in the beginning, that it felt like I was reinventing the wheel in order to get things done.

If it has been done by other small business owners before you, then there must also be some system or service that you can avail yourself of to do some of the things you may have no talent, knowledge, or desire to do. If you can find the support you need, so you're not distracted and drained from having to learn a whole new set of skills in addition to those required to getting your new business going, it makes good business sense to invest in such a service or system.

More concretely, I am speaking of developing employee and procedural manuals, payroll needs, guest tracking and data services. These are but a few of the elements of back office/behind the scenes needs important to the daily operation of your business.

I'm a huge fan of the resources available through www.RestaurantOwner.com and Royalty Rewards©. As mentioned previously, Royalty Rewards© is a superior database management and loyalty program. I not only end up saving money each year using this service, but I actually generate increased revenue by participating in this program. I cannot recommend it enough.

On the more nuts and bolts operational side of restaurant ownership are the resources found on www.RestaurantOwner.com. Here you'll discover manuals, templates, applications, and other business related items that will keep you from having to come up with something on your own.

There are other sites and resources out there, but these are the two I've found to be the most comprehensive and helpful for our needs. Remember running a business is a series of compromises and investments, of which perhaps the most important to always consider is the investment of your physical time versus a financial investment or system to preserve your physical time for investment elsewhere.

Mistake #48:   Great minds do think alike but you're not a Mastermind...yet.

I T IS OFTEN SAID if you want to be better than you are or reach for a higher position/greater success, then you need to surround yourself with individuals who emulate, live and will support the level of success you want to attain. More simply put: you need to hang with people who've attained the level of success you want or have surpassed it.

Among the many ideas presented in this book, this is one of the most important that can make your business grow and it has borne out significant truth in mine. A small word of caution here first. While this can and will provide you with the next level of success it will require you to prioritize how, when and where you spend your money. This can prove to be the most significant personal and business investment you make. You may have to forego the daily lattés. Speaking from experience, this is the single most important step I've ever taken to grow both personally and professionally. We all know the expression, *"You've got to break a couple of eggs to make an omelet."*

The concept of being a mastermind was mentioned in the famous Napoleon Hill book, *Think and Grow Rich.* Sounds really cool, doesn't it? Well it is. For the sake of your success, having someone or a group of people to bounce ideas off of is very important. Life does not happen in a vacuum, and while you may want to be the smartest person in the room, you only see through a glass darkly most of the time.

There is a concept out there known as "critical friends". These are people who you trust to share ideas with and are not going to fan your ego (or the lump you sit on) by simply being "yes men". In other words, a critical friend is someone you trust to tell you the truth and be critical of your ideas for the sake of helping refine them, point out the possible pitfalls, and focus you to save time, energy, and money. These folks are not deliberately contrarian and are the kind of people you want to have around.

In a Mastermind group, you may find yourself around 10-50 people who will invariably ask you tough critical questions you may not want to ask yourself. Aside from your personal daily group of critical friends, a Mastermind group is more or less going to be merciless. These are generally individuals with some proven track record of success as business owners and while they may not be in exactly your line of work, the skills, ideas, and outcomes can in most cases be applied directly.

You may be a novice in one of these groups or you may have been, or you are currently involved in one but have been a silent observer for a long time. Participation is mandatory. While listening is a critical skill, you will need to open your mouth and speak, interact, and let your ideas be heard. You may not feel qualified at first. If you find yourself thinking an idea may work and you've given considerable thought to the notion, then it is advisable you give air to it. I am not suggesting you constantly spew forth stuff for the sake of speaking: to the contrary. I support the idea of you growing in confidence building a solid foundation on which inspiration will come. This can be hastened while you're in a room with all these other people looking for the same thing you are: success.

As mentioned at the outset there is a cost for involvement in a Mastermind group. While you could potentially save money and start one locally, you will be much better off seeking out one run professionally, especially at first. Unless you're planning on running one of these groups full time and you possess the resources to be able to do all that is required to run a Mastermind group well, leave it to those who have already established themselves in this particular niche.

As previously mentioned the Mastermind group my wife and I belong to costs about $10,000 a year and meets three times per year. You can well imagine this was a very difficult expense for me to relate to as I couldn't see the end results at the beginning. I was skeptical to say the least. In addition to the base yearly expense there were the added costs of travel, lodging, and the minor terror of having to leave my growing business unattended and in the hands of others while I was away. Do you get the idea? Are you feeling a bit dizzy by the thought of going down this road?

The Mastermind group we belong to has other benefits included in the yearly membership. Among these are a monthly newsletter, monthly conference call, one-to-one coaching, and a private posting board/forum on their website. So while you may only be meeting face-to-face three times per year there can be opportunities to have other "touch stones" along the way.

Having these way points between meetings is extremely helpful and has contributed to preserving our sanity during some rough moments.

Further, we are tasked with "assignments" between groups, some of which become competitions/contests within the group. The members of the group are the judges. Over the past few years, my wife and I have walked away with paid vacations for the ideas we've come up with that were also ultimately very successful for our business in-between. Talk about a win-win situation. The group meetings inspired us to come up with a new promotion or advertising campaign which we put into use and then it won us a vacation. How can you go wrong with success breeding success?

To say joining our Mastermind group was one of the best things we've done for our business would be a mild understatement. As a result of being very proactively involved in the process, both in the group and then in our business, my wife and I have been able to garner a tremendous amount of credibility for the things we've put into place. This credibility has now afforded us the opportunity to develop a growing consulting business to both new and long standing restaurant and service business owners to improve the wide spectrum of components that make for a successful operation. This book is just one outgrowth of participating in the Mastermind process.

To learn about the Mastermind group that turned it all around for us, please email us at help@50mistakes.com and put the word "Mastermind" in the subject line.

Mistake #49: Your job description has become a monster growing out of control. You need to learn to trust your staff.

IN THE BEGINNING ESPECIALLY, my wife and I were control freaks and for the longest time would have rather done something ourselves than let anyone else in on the fun. Honestly, the adage, "If you want something done right do it yourself" rang true for us for the longest time. Then it all began to change for me. I woke up one day and realized that I didn't open a restaurant to give myself a job. I opened a restaurant to create jobs for others. This revelation made me have to rethink our entire owner/manager model of operation.

Don't let the following bloat your ego, but there is a great truth in the following statement. You, yes, you, had/have the foresight, guts, and initiative to gather the resources to start your own business. You may very well be a control freak, like we were. You are the "expert" in some area of your restaurant, be it chef, front of house, advertising. (In truth, you need to be expert in all areas, but as previously mentioned you also need to know when to ask for help.) You are the one with the guts in launching your dream. This alone puts you ahead of most of the staff you will hire, as they may never find that kind of courage. To be clear: This is NOT a put down or insult, just simply a statement of reality. Not everyone is cut out to be a business owner and many would rather work for someone else, than be in the position of having to make decisions.

You need to humbly wrap your head around the foregoing. This shift in perspective is hopefully triggering a whole new set of thoughts for you.

Your staff needs to run the day-to-day operational aspects of your business so it frees you up to grow your business. You need to be able to train your front of house staff in the ethos and nuts and bolts of how you want to present your establishment to the community. You might train one or two of your staff to conduct inventory and do some ordering. Everyone who works front of house needs to know your guest relations/guest concerns/guest handling policies so you become the last word and the last line, not necessarily the first. You also, need to appropriately compensate the staff you task with the added responsibilities that relieve you of the day-to-day burdens. Recall, you're building long term stability and loyalty for your investment.

Borrowing a thought from the education world: students will rise to the expectations of their teacher. If the expectations are set too low, the students will not grow. If the expectations are set too high, the students will not succeed, unless, the teacher is equipped with the skills to break down the high goal in realistic steps and time frame so success can be obtained.

By virtue of your initiative and leadership in opening a business, you place yourself in the position of being a teacher. Your goal is to target the apparent skill sets of each of your staff and grow them to their fullest potential so in the ideal your staff collectively represents who you are. You want them to become a well-coordinated and well-orchestrated team. In simple terms…your goal is to replicate yourself in your staff so the job(s) gets done.

In order to accomplish what I'm suggesting, you need to let go of the control and have patience, while planning on failures, snags, and inconveniences to happen along the way. Given the opportunity, many individuals will happily and voluntarily step up to the plate and take on more responsibility. You need to create an environment where this can happen.

My wife and I have grown quite a bit over the years we've been in business and are blessed to have learned how to trust our staff. We've been able to provide our staff with opportunities other restaurant owners wouldn't even consider. In general, we can honestly say our staff is fiercely loyal. We've been able to send them, on our behalf, to a trade show or two, to wine and spirit tastings, and even local chamber of commerce meetings.

My wife, my family, and I have benefited significantly from what we've been able to create. We're able to attend our Mastermind group three times per year, take our children on vacation and/or steal away a few nights ourselves, and even take off some Friday and Saturday nights. We carve out time every day for exercise.

Don't be lulled into complacency or dreaminess here. There have been more than a few weekends where our plans had to be cancelled because we were unexpectedly, though very happily slammed by a busy night. It's our business and our responsibility and to get here has taken a great deal of work, which has been well worth it.

Mistake #50: You're at the bottom of your own list. You need to refill your own cup.

WE ARE ALL FAMILIAR with the old saw, "All work and no play makes Jack a dull boy." Are you a dull Jack? Certainly, no one wants to be around a dull Jack and I'm nearly 100% positive you aren't going to last over the long haul if you don't set apart time to rejuvenate yourself. Life is too short and time goes by way too quickly. You must be able to prioritize your life in such a way that it allows you time to disconnect and take care of personal needs.

Much of what has been detailed up to this point will hopefully afford you the opportunity to have time. Along the way, you may need to actually schedule time for yourself as if it were a business meeting you can't afford to miss. This means you will need to schedule the time for yourself as part of your daily and/or weekly routine.

Remember your goal, if it wasn't a conscious one prior to reading this book, should be one now: You're in business to provide a job for others, not for yourself. You want to create a lifestyle because of your business so you're not a slave to it.

I hope by getting this far in my book, you've come to realize having a broader goal for your life outside of your business is an extraordinary motivator. I want to see you succeed to the point that you can take time to go on vacation with your family because you've selected, trained, and provided the opportunities for your staff to demonstrate their enthusiasm, dedication, and trustworthiness so you can feel comfortable leaving them to run things for an extended period of time.

To get to this point will take careful planning and well placed effort on your part. It is a thoroughly attainable goal. Let's get you there.

Made in the USA
Columbia, SC
08 November 2018